T0178790

# Handbook of Artificial Intelligence and Robotic Process Automation

# Handbook of Artificial Intelligence and Robotic Process Automation

## Policy and Government Applications

Edited by

Al Naqvi and J. Mark Munoz

ANTHEM PRESS

Anthem Press
An imprint of Wimbledon Publishing Company
*www.anthempress.com*

This edition first published in UK and USA 2020
by ANTHEM PRESS
75–76 Blackfriars Road, London SE1 8HA, UK
or PO Box 9779, London SW19 7ZG, UK
and
244 Madison Ave #116, New York, NY 10016, USA

*British Library Cataloguing-in-Publication Data*
A catalogue record for this book is available from the British Library.

ISBN-13: 978-1-78527-495-4 (Hbk)
ISBN-10: 1-78527-495-3 (Hbk)

This title is also available as an e-book.

# CONTENTS

# ILLUSTRATIONS

**Figures**

**Tables**

# Chapter 1

# INTRODUCTION

## J. Mark Munoz and Al Naqvi

President Vladimir Putin of Russia was not hedging when he stated that the country that advances in artificial intelligence (AI) will rule the world. Neither was President Xi of China who has set the goal for China to become a global leader in AI. Europe, Canada, the United States, and other major economies of the world have already understood that the dawn of a new era has begun. The advanced economies also understand that unlike previous revolutions, this new era offers little or no examples of how to maneuver and navigate through this technological and economic puzzle. The glorious rise of intelligent machines is not an ordinary change. After all, the last time humans lived with an intelligent species was when Neanderthals and humans coexisted and that didn't work out too well for the Neanderthals. Fast forward thousands of years and once again humanity is challenged by another type of intelligence. This time however, it is our own creation. Throughout human history, machines have stayed as loyal and subservient servants to the commands of their creator master. Today, the advent of AI is poised to change all that.

The previous paragraph captures the essence of the challenge: humans are creating intelligence but have no experience in dealing with intelligent machines. However, the change is not limited to machines. It encapsulates the massive social, political, economic, psychological, and spiritual alteration that comes with an extraordinary change. In some ways, the essence of humankind is being redefined. This book is about that change, but it is written from the perspective of government. Unlike dozens of texts that have addressed the change from a business side, this is the first book that will address the role, responsibility, and challenge of managing AI from the government side.

In some ways, the advent of AI technology happened too soon and too unexpectedly. It is as if terminator robots and AI bots jumped out of a Hollywood flick and started breeding furiously. Within a seven-year period, the fascinating stories that ornamented comic books suddenly became the ultimate priorities of company boards and government leaders. Flash crashes in financial markets triggered by bot traders and bot armies invading democratic institutions became bleeding headlines. Institutions collapsed under the assaults of smart bots and companies crumbled as cyber warriors pierced through their firewalls. Individuals surrendered their rationality and judgment to the onslaught of opinion bots. As populist movements swept across the world, data-bots masterfully conquered the emotional spaces of the innocent victims and realigned psychological constructs and ideological structures of helpless humans. They didn't know what hit them. Hate spewed from multiple directions as bot armies were used to sway public opinion, and a sense of powerlessness took shape in human civilization. The important factor to note is that all of this happened in a matter of less than a decade, in technologically advanced economies, and with the machines that humans had built themselves.

The world was not prepared for such an enormous change. As soon as the world grasped the enormity of the challenge and what it meant, visionary and responsible governments scrambled to make sense of the dynamic and uncontrollable change. The White House issued multiple reports and formed task forces. The US Senate and Congress launched hearings. The European Union established policies and frameworks to deal with the enormity of the challenge. China launched multibillion dollar programs. Russia tried to take a central position in the transformation. Canada designated entire cities to create the AI revolution.

As large, economically prosperous, and technologically advanced countries established growth and governance programs (the two G's central to the AI revolution), some not so technologically advanced high-GDP countries followed with establishing ministries and focus areas on AI. Consider this dilemma: When large and technologically advanced countries are having a hard time to adjust to the aftershocks of the AI technology, what hope remains for the over a hundred governments that have not even started to consider what it means to be in the midst of the most transformative technological eye of the storm?

At the intersection of opportunism and fear, a sense of sober acceptance is emerging. Governments are beginning to understand the urgency and enormity of change. This book is their first comprehensive guide of what to do and how to do it. This book is a guide for leadership as much as it is a "how to" manual for government leaders.

From learning how to deploy the AI technology to modernize and transform the government to learning how to launch a national AI transformation program, this book has it all. As the first guide for all types of governments—small, large, developed, underdeveloped—this book takes you on a journey that will help in reducing the transformation cost to the society. It will return control back to the humans and help alleviate and reduce the chaos that has emerged just in the infancy stage of this revolution.

Beyond the obvious two G questions (Growth and Governance) it should not be forgotten that AI is just as much an economic and social transformation as it is a military technological change. On the one hand it will redefine what it means to work, transform employment, restructure institutions, and reorient human civilization to a different course. On the other, it will create sophisticated combat machines designed for merciless killing. On the one hand we will strive to solve human problems. On the other, we will create the finest killing machines humankind has ever known.

And this defines yet another dilemma for governments. How to come together to address the problem of AI-based weaponization? This book also addresses that critical aspect of governmental responsibility.

The bottom line is that if governments don't invest in AI, they will miss out on the most critical and transformative times in human history. The goddess of competition will crown other countries as global leaders and the traditional leaders will vanish and collapse in a fashion familiar to students of history. If they do invest and innovate, then how should they do it responsibly so as to make the world less dangerous and more accommodating? This book provides powerful answers to these questions.

The traditional order has been challenged. The advent of AI and robotic process automation (RPA) has threatened many jobs, reconfigured economic frameworks, and forced governments to think in new ways.

For some governments around the world, AI and RPA are the new normal and the pressure is on finding a suitable balance between tradition and technology. And for others the whole AI transformation continues to be a vague and ambiguous pursuit. They remain oblivious to the fact that their countries could soon turn into ghost towns as AI will alter the trade and reconfigure the global trade network.

The economic impact of AI and RPA cannot be denied. AI impacts productivity and overall GDP (PWC, 2016). Nesbitt (2017) indicated that AI impacts trade by: (1) enabling supply chains, (2) creating efficiency in compliance software, (3) speeding up and creating better contracts, and (4) improving access to finance.

These changes can also be a threat to many economies. A recent report from Ball State University showed that in the United States almost 9 out of 10 jobs were lost to robots and not to trade (Hicks and Devaraj, 2015). New technologies threaten about 40 percent of jobs in the United States and approximately two-thirds of those in the developing world (Gershon, 2017).

Industries need to work around challenges brought about by AI. Barriers organizations have to overcome relating to AI include: concerns over data protection and privacy, consumer trust and regulatory acceptance, building relevant technologies, managing the volume of unstructured data, optimizing supply chain and production systems, and overcoming potentially high investment (PWC, 2016).

While challenges and threats exist, so do opportunities. A few examples are shown below:

**Industrial improvement**. Several industries are poised to benefit from AI: Healthcare (data-based diagnostic support), Automotive (autonomous fleets for ride sharing), Financial Services (personalized financial planning), Retail and Consumer (personalized design and production), Technology, Communication, and Entertainment (media archiving and search), Manufacturing (enhanced monitoring and autocorrection), Energy (smart meters), and Transport and Logistics (autonomous trucking) (PWC, 2016).

**Productivity gains**. AI enables productivity enhancement, changes work processes, and can create jobs (Rao, 2017).

**Economic growth**. The countries projected to have the highest AI gains are China (26 percent GDP boost) and North America (14.5 percent GDP boost), with a total of 70 percent of the estimated $10.7 trillion global economic impact (PWC, 2016).

**Expansion in entrepreneurship**. There were about 1,500 AI-related start-ups in the United States in 2016, receiving funding of around $5 billion (Rao, 2017).

With the strong influence of AI in industry and governments, an organization's ability to manage and navigate change is critical. AI will set the stage for economic transformation and disruption and will be the foundation for new competitive advantages (PWC, 2016).

Some governments have started to implement strategic measures to gain an advantage in AI. The United Arab Emirates appointed a minister of AI to strategically prepare the country for technological advancements in the field (Wendel, 2017). Singapore is aiming to be a pioneer as a smart nation where technology is merged with the way of life of all residents (Vaswani, 2017).

The objective of this book is to gather the viewpoints of experts and thought leaders from around the world and share their ideas on the implications and impact of AI on governments. With scarce literature on the topic, this groundbreaking book aims to be an important resource for think tanks, consulting companies, international organizations, policy makers, and government officials worldwide.

This book expands the understanding of AI and RPA at different levels. In the academic front, scholars and researchers would find the content useful in furthering their research agenda. Consulting firms would find value on fresh insights relating to AI. Entrepreneurs will have an enhanced understanding on the relationship between industry and government in the context of AI. Government officials will learn strategic approaches pertaining to the advancement of AI in their countries. The authors hope that these ideas will stimulate discussion and debate in order that solutions to problems may be found and gateways to success will be uncovered.

The book is organized in such a way that the reader is exposed to diverse topics relating to AI and relevant government functions and operations. The goal is not only to educate the reader on AI and RPA but also to set the foundation for excellence in government operations in a fast-paced, technology-driven world.

The book has 14 chapters: Chapter 1, Introduction (*J. Mark Munoz and Al Naqvi*); Part I: Strategic Frameworks of AI, Chapter 2, Neuralization: How to Build AI Country Strategy? (*Al Naqvi*); Chapter 3, Global Governance of Artificial Intelligence (*Nicolas Miailhe and Yolanda Lannquist*); Chapter 4, Government 4.0 and Evidence-Based Policies: AI and Data Analytics to the Rescue (*Nathalie de Marcellis-Warin and Thierry Warin*); Chapter 5, The Strategic Implications of Artificial Intelligence for International Security (*Jean-Marc Ricli*); Part II: AI and Economic Development, Chapter 6, Using AI to Improve Economic Productivity: A Business Model Perspective (*Oleksiy Osiyevskyy, Yongjian Bao, and Carlos M. DaSilva*); Chapter 7, Handling Resultant Unemployment from Artificial Intelligence (*Margaret A. Goralski and Krystyna Górniak-Kocikowska*); Chapter 8, Building Tech Zones to Enhance AI (*Melodena Stephens Balakrishnan*); Part III: AI and the Enhancement of Governance, Chapter 9, AI-Government versus E-government: How to Reinvent Government with AI? (*Al Naqvi*); Chapter 10, Economic Governance When Humans and AI Are at Work (*Dirk Nicolas Wagner*); Chapter 11, Legal Systems at a Crossroads: Justice in the Age of Artificial Intelligence (*Nicolas Economou and Bruce Hedin*); Chapter 12, The Curious Case of Fake News: Fighting Smart Machiavellian Machines (*Daniel Lemus-Delgado and Armando López-Cuevas*); Chapter 13, Applications of Artificial Intelligence and RPA to Improve Government Performance (*Luis Soto and Sergio Biggemann*); and Chapter 14, Conclusion (*J. Mark Munoz and Al Naqvi*).

AI and RPA have transformed many industries worldwide. These collective transformations reshaped economic frameworks and therefore have had an impact on governments. The way a government manages AI will define its competitive advantage. The chapters in this book offer the latest research and strategic approaches that industries and governments can consider when planning its future course.

## References

Gershon, L. (2017). The automation resistant skills we should nurture. BBC. Accessed September 20, 2017. Available at: http://www.bbc.com/capital/story/20170726-the-automation-resistant-skills-we-should-nurture.

Hicks, M. J., and Devaraj, S. (2015). *The myth and reality of manufacturing in America* [online]. Available at: http://conexus.cberdata.org/files/MfgReality.pdf%0D.

Nesbitt, J. (2017). 4 ways artificial intelligence is transforming trade. Accessed September 21, 2017. Available at: http://www.tradeready.ca/2017/topics/import-export-trade-management/4-ways-artificial-intelligence-transforming-trade/.

PWC (2016). Sizing the prize. PWC's Global Artificial Intelligence Study: Exploiting the AI Revolution. Accessed September 21, 2017. Available at: https://www.pwc.com/gx/en/issues/data-and-analytics/publications/artificial-intelligence-study.html.

Rao, A. (2017). A strategist's guide to artificial intelligence. Strategy + Business. Accessed September 20, 2017. Available at: https://www.strategy-business.com/article/A-Strategists-Guide-to-Artificial-Intelligence?gko=0abb5&utm_source=itw&utm_medium=20170523&utm_campaign=respB.

Vaswani, K. (2017). Tomorrow's cities: Singapore's plans for a smart nation. BBC. Accessed September 20, 2017. Available at: http://www.bbc.com/news/technology-39641262.

Wendel, S. (2017). U.A.E. appoints minister of artificial intelligence in cabinet reshuffle. Accessed May 24, 2018. Available at: https://www.forbesmiddleeast.com/en/u-a-e-appoints-minister-of-artificial-intelligence-in-cabinet-reshuffle/.

# Part I
# STRATEGIC FRAMEWORKS OF AI

# Chapter 2

# NEURALIZATION: HOW TO BUILD AI COUNTRY STRATEGY?

## Al Naqvi

There is little doubt that humankind has entered a new era of progress, prosperity, and peril. The advent and rise of artificial intelligence (AI) have altered the concept of machines by transitioning them from human-controlled to intelligent and autonomous (Makridakis 2017). While there is little doubt that AI is transforming all aspects of human life, and most government executives understand the importance of adopting the AI technology, the approach used to embrace the AI technology is ineffective and even dysfunctional. First, it is patterned after the old e-government-era paradigm and assumes that AI is simply the extension of the e-age. Second, it is use-case-centric where departments and agencies are developing point solutions and applications as one-off solutions without them being part of some broader strategic framework. Third, while governments—even of large countries—have launched webpages and organized conferences on the AI revolution, no formal body of knowledge, frameworks, or models exist on how to develop a strategic plan for an entire country. Many of those efforts are superficial or too tactical. This chapter develops the first such strategic model. Finally, while government executives want to take an ownership role in leading the transformation, they just don't know how, and this chapter helps them to develop that perspective.

## First, a Primer on Neuralization

AI, unlike all previous innovations made by humans, is unique. It is the automation of total work performed by humans—that is, automation of both cognitive and physical elements of work. On the physical end of the work domain, we are familiar with the potential of cars, airplanes, boats, submarines, and so on. They enable humans to reach remarkable physical capability that is far beyond the physiological capability of a human. A similar impact or scaling on the cognitive side implies a supercharged human brain. While the physical automation can be compared to muscular or structural elements of a human, cognitive capabilities are like the neural system that controls human progress throughout the lifetime of a human individual and on a collective basis guides the course of the human civilization. The nervous system helps solve problems; provides learning on how to deal with the surrounding environment, survive, create, develop goals; and many other things that are uniquely human. It also provides the support behind the physical apparatus (muscles, physical body) for balance, dexterity, and other things that make physical movement possible and controllable. Just as physical work automation (e.g., automobiles) augmented the human capability to discover, explore, conquer, and exploit beyond our wildest imagination, the cognitive augmentation enabled by AI will help humans to do that on a much boarder scale. Physical work automation enabled us to cut through mountains, conquer seas, or journey to the moon. Being able to discover, explore, conquer, and exploit the depths of the human mind, human societies, economics, and political structures on the one hand and accelerating the discovery in science and technology on the other will create a never-seen-before powerful and revolutionary thrust.

In this new setting, the change element is the "neuralization" of the human society. Neuralization, in this context, implies the development of intelligence (ability to comprehend information, formulate goals, act, etc.) that resides outside of naturally occurring intelligence in humans. The neuralization of the human civilization is the greatest power ever unleashed. It means that in addition to the human mind, other autonomous and intelligent entities will thrive and develop. It also means that knowledge and data that have always been captured for human use will now have another consumer.

Thus, when the analogy of electricity is used for AI, it implies that AI will become the energy that will enable and drive all other progress in the world. Given the power of this technology, it is essential that proper planning, strategy, investment, and other such tools are employed at the highest echelons of government, but we don't see that happening. Only few countries have created AI offices. Many such offices are not part of the cabinet or a ministry and are placed under existing science or technology offices. In cases where such groups are part of the government, they act more or less as extended marketing arms of tech giants (large tech companies). These departments do not engage in rigorous planning activities as performed by more established agencies and departments. Many don't know how to even start the strategy development process. In some cases, the preferred method by such departments is to have tech giants organize conferences and have large consulting firms develop some marketing material. The conferences turn out to be either technology focused (i.e., discussion of algorithms) or happy stories where budding entrepreneurs display how they are developing technologies. Strategic rigor, robustness, and comprehensiveness are mostly missing. The strategic plans mostly lay out broad research initiatives and that's where they stop. Actual plans with measurable results and clear objectives are not created. Despite acknowledging the revolutionary impact of AI, the approach of most countries in managing the AI transformation is too casual and clueless.

It is not unusual to have that mindset. While electric power distribution began in the late 1800s and nuclear technology in the 1940s, the US Department of Energy was created in 1977 and that too only after America experienced its worst energy crisis. For nearly a century, government lacked the vision to view energy as the core driving force of the economy, and it took a major crisis to help identify the need for managing energy. Today, even after almost 140 years of the power distribution, 67 percent of the developing world population does not have access to electric power. Early planning and strategic thinking can help bring capabilities in developing countries and also ensure that developed countries can avoid major catastrophes.

The developed countries are approaching the AI revolution as an emerging research area and not as a rapidly maturing national or global industry. Countries have yet to recognise that the amplification of intelligence will happen at multiple levels, for example, at an individual level, at a systems level, and then at a superintelligence level. The interaction across these levels will give rise to unpredictable emergent dynamics, real-time systems, and feedback loops. This will lead to major structural changes across all human affairs (social, political, economic, others). For example, we are already seeing signs of such emergent behavior with flash crash in stock markets. With neuralization, we are creating and deploying intelligent nodes in an already established network of relationships with its own configuration. Such nodes will create new and different interactions and can lead to unpredictable dynamics. Planning for the AI revolution is no trivial task and it should be taken extremely seriously.

For example, the strategic plan for AI in the United States is research focused and it resulted from a request for information (RFI) that received input only from about fifty entities (US Government 2019). They were mostly obtained from input received from a few consulting firms, some tech giants, and only a handful of universities. In 2016, under the Obama administration, another RFI collected similar information and in that as well, the participation was low.

In this chapter, as I explain how to formulate the strategic plan for a country, I strongly recommend that countries must consider deploying ministries, cabinet positions, and agencies to lead and manage this transformation. Such a ministry or agency will be critical—and parallel to the other agencies such as the Department of Energy.

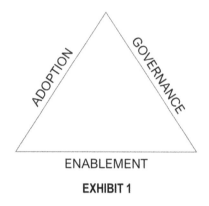

ENABLEMENT

**EXHIBIT 1**

**Figure 2.1** The three roles of government.

## The Three Roles of Government

As the AI revolution solidifies, a government has three roles to play in leading the AI transformation. These three roles lead to the development of interdependent capabilities that must be pursued simultaneously (Figure 2.1). The three roles are as follows:

**Enabler:** In the enabler role the government develops capabilities that help engineer and accelerate innovation and growth in AI. This is done by supporting private sector and academic institutions, nonprofits, and other research-centric institutions. This is what will maintain the competitive edge of a country. From intelligent automation in manufacturing to the services sector, from logistics to research, the competitive edge of a country will greatly depend upon its ability to adopt AI. With AI, countries can not only improve their existing industries but also design and develop new sectors and industries.

**Adopter:** In the adopter role, the government adopts AI for military and citizen support services—as well as to run all operations and functions of the government. This is done to keep the government efficient, effective, and relevant for citizens. It is also embraced to foster national security. As governments adopt AI, they become more efficient, more effective, more citizen friendly, and more relevant. Note that it is possible that governments can adopt AI without achieving any improvements or results—however, that is not what is desirable.

**Governance:** In the governance role, a government ensures that the adoption and dissemination of AI technology lead to creating a better world for humans. This is the traditional role of government, which will include policy, regulations, and guidelines to ensure that AI is responsibly adopted and disseminated in the society.

A government must play all three roles simultaneously and coordinate activities across them. These three roles are interdependent and not pursuing them will expose a country to significant risks.

## Understanding the Risks

The risks of not pursuing these three roles simultaneously are presented below:

**Adoption without Enablement:** When a government adopts AI but without encouraging and supporting domestic development of technology (i.e., enabling), it exposes itself to several risks. First, this implies that the government will be dependent upon foreign-developed technology, and since AI systems are far less understood than non-AI systems, the risk of foreign intervention increases significantly. It also establishes permanent dependency. Second, unlike non-AI systems, AI systems are not configurable systems. They are dependent upon the data available and the algorithms that perform best with the available data. Without a domestic industry, a country will necessarily have to release its data to foreign entities. Lastly, without enablement, a country will lose its competitive advantage.

**Adoption without Governance:** When a government adopts AI but does not play a role in governing its development, deployment, and design, it exposes itself to losing its grip on several important aspects of the AI technology. First, it becomes impossible to know if the artifacts introduced in government are safe and stable. Second, governments will need advance notice of upcoming challenges like unemployment. Third, when something bad happens rapid intervention can take place—for example, a stock market flash crash. Fourth, technology interaction can enable unpredictable paths. Fifth, a government can become oppressive, dysfunctional, or autocratic. Sixth, a government would not know when it is being manipulated. Neither the excitement of technology nor pressure from large companies should be used as excuses to not implement governance.

**Governance without Adoption:** A government can develop, propose, debate, and apply all kinds of rigorous standards about AI, but if it fails to adopt AI it will soon discover that unlike other technologies, AI cannot be monitored or governed by passing laws. Governing AI will require the simultaneous development and deployment of AI technologies to monitor other AI technologies. This interdependent and recursive nature of technology requires that a government adopt technology that it wants to govern.

**Governance without Enablement:** Enablement implies strengthening the private sector and academic research community in a country to develop, design, and invent new AI products and services. As with government adoption, having governance without enablement will not help much. To monitor and govern AI, governments would need something to be governed. If there are no technologies to be governed, it makes no sense to develop governance, unless the focus is on the governance of foreign-developed systems. Many of the governance systems would also come from the private sector, research institutions, and academia.

**Enablement without Governance:** Perhaps the most dangerous situation—and one that is developing now—is the ungoverned development and proliferation of AI technology. As the AI technology is enabled in the private sector and research centers across the world, and there is no supporting governance infrastructure or technologies, the risk to human civilization is maximized.

**Enablement without Adoption:** When technology is developed in the private sector and academia, and government fails to adopt it promptly, several undesirable consequences will result. First, government's slow adoption means that citizens fail to take full advantage of services. Second, government lags in providing support for the private sector. Third, government fails to take full advantage of enablement.

### Building the Strategy: The Framework

Building the country strategy requires three coordinated activities (Figure 2.2):

1. Vertical Mapping
2. Horizontal Mapping
3. Cognitive Scaling

### *Vertical Mapping*

In Vertical Mapping, a government establishes its core strategy about each of its specific roles of Enablement, Adoption, and Governance. Vertical Mapping is performed with the mindset that AI will necessarily alter the structures of existing industries. The twentieth-century strategy models were designed where natural boundaries of industries and sectors were preserved. The AI revolution will make things much more fluid where the sector boundaries will be breached and cross-sector processes (and firms) will replace the existing sector-specific structures. Sectors will lose their current structures and become far more malleable. As such, instead of focusing on sector boundaries, Vertical Mapping focuses on processes.

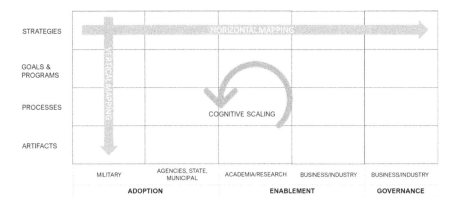

**Figure 2.2** Strategy canvas for country strategy.

The strategy development method is composed of setting specific mission and objectives, formulating goals, and identifying new processes and the artifacts needed to create the transformation. For example, in the military adoption role, the government will develop a clear objective for embedding intelligence in offensive and defensive weapon systems, in controlling and coordinating combat-related activities, in using AI for noncombat-related services, in gathering and acting upon intelligence, and in cybersecurity. Since countries compete for global dominance, a strategy must consider the actions of the competitor or adversary. The drivers of strategy must include competitive actions, competitive advantage, capabilities, priorities, investment and return relationships, national security and citizen-related goals, and other considerations. Vertical Mapping will identify key processes not only within a branch (e.g., Army, Navy, Air Force) but also across various branches. The products and services within and across branches are identified.

For Vertical Mapping, in government agencies, state, and city governments, goals are set at the highest level and then objectives and projects are defined at each agency level, while ensuring that cross-agency goals are set. Capabilities developed in one agency can be used in another agency. Since most of the activities undertaken by various states are similar, coordination and collaboration across states can help create powerful results. In AI solutions, more data is often good and hence collaboration across agencies and states to get more data for specific solutions will lead to better systems and higher return on investment.

Once overall strategies are determined, the Vertical Mappings move from top to bottom and then bottom-up, oscillating constantly until the plan is fully developed (Figure 2.3). The movement happens when strategies are broken

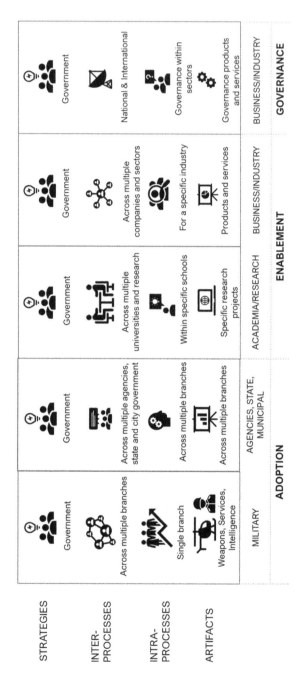

**Figure 2.3** Country strategy development.

down into interagency or interorganizational processes, and interorganizational processes are segmented into intraorganizational processes, which are segmented into specific artifacts.

The government-level goals are clarified and designed to improve the functioning of the entire government. The focus remains on optimizing the three roles of the government.

*Interagency Processes* focus on developing capabilities across agencies and branches. They refer to various processes within an agency or branch. *Artifacts* implies the products and services (self-contained intelligent agents). Cascading interagency processes establish the road map for products and services. Each of the artifacts and processes is further expanded to show value maps and is tied to a program.

## Horizontal Mapping

The Horizontal Mapping links the capabilities across the various roles of government such that capabilities developed in one area can be made available to another area. It also includes developing best practices across all roles. If Vertical Mapping was focused on identifying opportunities and developing visions and plans, Horizontal Mapping answers the questions of how to execute in a way that meaningful benefits accrue fast and the downside of technological revolutions is avoided. It implies that the government ensures that it is making progress in all vertical areas and doing it efficiently and effectively and that such progress is simultaneous and has a positive impact on various aspects of human life.

Horizontal Mapping ensures the following:

1. The datasets are recognized and made available, and data quality is ensured.
2. Dataset access is not limited to tech giants and smaller and midsized firms also have access to data (using the electricity theme, not allowing data access to all will be analogous to restricting electricity to only large companies and monopolies).
3. Algorithms and their use across multiple verticals are tracked and knowledge about their efficiency, use, and performance is shared.
4. Impact of all AI artifacts and processes developed in the verticals is analyzed for their impact on human behavior. Specifically, the impact on human psychological states and behavior is analyzed when interacting with such technologies. For example, if a human applies for a job and her first interview is with a robot, her dignity and self-image as a human may get impacted in a certain way. It is important to understand that impact.

5. The impact of all artifacts and processes on other systems should be understood. This includes understanding the behavior and interactions of all systems that an artifact interacts with.
6. The interaction of intelligent systems is understood, and their interactive dynamics studied. Opportunities of real-time systems with feedback loops, for example, swarm systems, and the potential of amplifying intelligence are thoroughly understood.
7. The Wheel of Impact is the assessment of verticals on various human-centric processes and institutions including economics, law, security, politics, business, and climate (Figure 2.4).
8. Managing the AI revolution requires building cross-functional capabilities in a country. Currently, the newly formed AI offices are focusing on developing AI talent, that is, data science experts who can help develop new technologies. This is not enough. Business leaders and functional area experts need to be just as involved and knowledgeable as their technology or data science experts. Without proper business sponsorship, backing, and leadership, companies and agencies will not be able to develop the most comprehensive and strong programs. Social scientists need to get involved and become part of the revolution.
9. Data, technology, and processing infrastructure are all considered as endowment. Datasets are important considerations, and developing, cultivating, nurturing, and curating datasets are critical activities. These activities are performed and managed as governments manage agricultural crops or energy.
10. Subsidies and incentives are planned for building and developing AI systems and managing data.

While vertical strategy ensures that progress is made across all the critical areas, the horizontal mapping ensures that such progress is optimized, and citizens are protected and served well.

### *Cognitive Scaling*

Cognitive Scaling is the way to ensure that competitive advantage of the country is maintained and enhanced. With Cognitive Scaling countries ensure that they build capabilities that are consistent with maximizing the competitive potential of the country. The intelligent infrastructure, as described above, of a country is viewed as nodes of a complex adaptive system.

Clusters of cross-sector and cross-industry capability building are identified and forecasted. Entire industries can face major structural changes, and some could be wiped out. The traditional moats do not protect industries from the

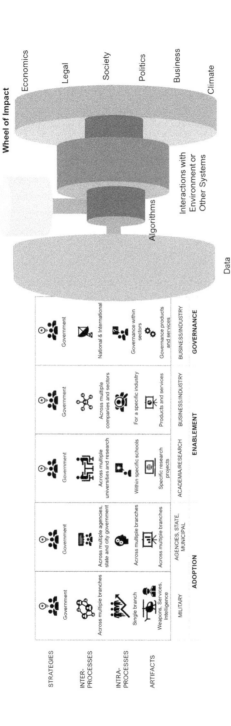

**Figure 2.4** Integrated governance and country strategy.

onslaught of AI-centric disruption. A technology firm can emerge as an automotive company, a financial services provider, or a hospital. The traditional focus on cluster development is only on cross-building of capabilities; however, with AI the focus needs to be on understanding the risks. Like colliding galaxies, entire sectors and industries can experience major structural changes. Such a massive change can have a significant impact on a country and its institutions. The concept of nation can change drastically (Bartlett 2016). Institutions can be weakened intentionally or unintentionally. Clusters will no longer be a result of planned activities but can be made and remade via emergent dynamics. Competitive dynamics across nations can be altered overnight.

As systems become more interactive and connected, the stability of systems can be compromised. The behavior can become unpredictable.

## Conclusion

As we formulate strategy for a country, we need to take a proactive and broad perspective. The strategy formulation process begins with understanding the three key roles of the government and recognizing that all three roles will require building AI capabilities. The first role is of Adoption. In this role government adopts the AI technology. The second role is of Enabler. In this role government helps build capabilities and adoption in the private sector, industry, research centers, civic organizations, and academia. In the third role of Governance, government ensures that the products, services, and processes are built that protect national security and citizens from the developments in other areas. For each one of these roles, strategists build three types of strategic frameworks. The first framework is known as Vertical Mapping and it focuses on developing hierarchical plans for each role of the government. It begins by developing mission statements and objectives and then viewing entities as composed of processes, and instead of planning for entities, the planning focuses on inter- and intraorganizational processes. Vertical Mapping goes down to the level of products and services. Vertical Mapping answers the question of what to do, and Horizontal Mapping addresses how to do it best. It includes several factors that focus on datasets, algorithms, intelligent entity interaction, and governance. Cognitive Scaling refers to the ability to monitor the performance of the system, establish performance measures, and try to meet the standards set.

# References

Bartlett, S. J. (2016) *The Case for Government by Artifical Intelligence* [online]. Available from: http://philpapers.org/archive/BARTCF-6.pdf. Accessed June 11, 2019.

Makridakis, S. (2017) *The Forthcoming Artificial Intelligence (AI) Revolution: Its Impact on Society and Firms The Forthcoming Artificial Intelligence (AI) Revolution: Its Impact on Society and Firms* [online]. Available from: https://hephaestus.nup.ac.cy/handle/11728/9254. Accessed June 4, 2019.

US Government (2019) *The National Artificial Intelligence Research and Development Strategic Plan: 2019 Update* [online]. Available from: https://www.nitrd.gov/pubs/National-AI-RD-Strategy-2019.pdf. Accessed December 2019.

# Chapter 3

# GLOBAL GOVERNANCE OF ARTIFICIAL INTELLIGENCE

Nicholas Miailhe and Yolanda Lannquist

Anchored in the wider digital revolution, artificial intelligence (AI) is poised to transform the economy, society, geopolitics, and the global political orders we know today. The AI revolution's impact inextricably combines very substantive opportunities (e.g., AI for Good) and serious societal risks (e.g., unemployment, bias, privacy, safety). The prospect to shape AI development toward capturing these opportunities and minimizing the risks will depend on national-level policy, industry practices, and international coordination and collaboration. However, a global governance approach must consider the unique dynamics and challenges present in AI development. This chapter presents some of the main challenges and dynamics in AI governance and novel global governance approaches to help ensure safe and inclusive AI that benefits society broadly.

## Complex Dynamics of the Rise of AI Today

### *Balance beneficial innovation with mitigating societal risks*

Governance approaches for AI must consider the complexity of striking the right balance between activating and supporting beneficial innovations and mitigating downside risks and adverse effects. Compounded with the urgency of issues faced by humanity today, such as rapid climate change, biodiversity degradation, and widespread global poverty, our problems are becoming increasingly complex in an interconnected global environment. As a "general-purpose technology,"[1] AI has the potential to boost innovation, productivity, and economic growth globally[2] and support progress toward the UN sustainable development goals (SDGs) and achieve other social and humanitarian milestones.[3] For example, in healthcare, privacy and security may be traded off for more accurate diagnostics and personalized treatment. In transportation, autonomous cars can reduce fatalities and carbon emissions while displacing millions of jobs. Satellite imagery for humanitarian planning balances privacy with access to humanitarian aid.

### *Policymakers lag in rapid technological advancement*

Lawmakers are increasingly unable to stay apprised and keep up with fast-paced technological trends. AI is highly systemic, complex, and volatile and its development is rapid and unpredictable. Policymakers are increasingly unable to stay up-to-date and to manage impacts and risks. Knowledge gaps in government and communication gaps between the government and technology sectors hamper smart policymaking. This can lead to even informed policymakers struggling to predict the impacts of policies.[4] While the course of technology and its impact is unpredictable, ex ante policy may sometimes be too rigid or not appropriate. Besides, timely policymaking is often hampered by slow consensus-based processes in democratic countries.

Moreover, policymakers are less able to monitor or regulate AI development and deployment because it is distributed across stakeholders (private sector, public sector, academia), across sectors in the economy, and across the globe in interconnected supply chains. Governance must also address small and medium enterprises (SMEs), corporates, public sector, nongovernmental organizations (NGOs), and nonprofits seeking to implement AI in their organizational processes for performance and efficiency gains.

### *Global AI race to the bottom?*

A global race is developing among firms and states to develop and deploy new AI technology as quickly as possible. In a highly competitive market, firms are incentivized to rapidly grow, innovate, and offer products to market. Lacking either market incentives or global coordination, this fast-paced competition can drive a "race to the bottom" in standards and precautions for ethics and safety.

It seems that the rise of AI within the digital industrial landscape strengthens the "winner-takes-all" market tendency, where companies offering the most advanced technologies quickly capture market domination because of economies of scale and network effects. This is exemplified by the current global market domination of American AI leaders GAFAMI (Google, Apple, Facebook, Amazon, Microsoft, and IBM) and Chinese AI leaders BHATX (Baidu, Huawei, Alibaba, Tencent, and Xiaomi). To capture these market gains, companies may bypass ethical and safety standards, testing procedures, and precautions. Safety and ethical precautions include ensuring inclusive and representative datasets, sufficient testing and impact assessment before deployment, precautions for data privacy and security, and providing pathways for auditing algorithms used in public agencies.

### *"Risk appetite" for innovation varies across countries*

Global governance approaches for AI will have to grapple with the inconsistencies among national-level regulatory frameworks and regimes. "Risk appetite" in the trade-off between regulation and innovation varies across countries, hampering global coordination. Some government, industry, and civil society leaders are more ready to sacrifice citizens' data, privacy, fair treatment, and safety. Consumers' tolerance for risk varies too, due not only to divergences in value systems but also to socioeconomic realities on the ground. For example, according to McKinsey & Company, 93 percent of Chinese customers are willing to share location data with their car manufacturer, compared to 65 percent of Germans and 72 percent of Americans.[5] Similarly, in a 2017 PwC study respondents in Africa were twice as willing to have a major surgery performed by an AI robot than respondents in Europe, even given present-day technological limitations.[6]

Moreover, lack of coordination can lead to competitive advantage for less regulated countries. Against the backdrop of a global race among private companies and states to develop AI technology, some states have been laxer than others in enforcing standards and precautions for ethics and safety. Countries more responsive to citizen and consumer demands for safety and privacy protection, including European states, may lag in AI innovation in the short term. Regulation, such as for data privacy and usage, can slow the rate and increase the costs of AI innovation and adoption. As an example, compared to less regulated markets such as the United States and China, the European General Data Protection Regulation (GDPR) may initially slow down access to valuable "training data" used to improve machine learning algorithms.

### *Fragmented international policy landscape*

Increasingly aware of strategic economic, political, and military issues at stake, national governments have released a series of policies and strategies aimed to boost national AI innovation relative to other nations. National economic interests are at stake, with the potential to capture financial and economic gains from new product offerings and markets. After the United States and Canada in 2016, China, the European Union, and several other countries have recently started to invest billions of dollars in toward the goal of becoming global AI leaders.[78] Lacking coordination, these strategies fail to benefit from opportunities to collaborate and share resources (e.g., data, models, and computing assets) and lessons (e.g., ethics, best practices).

In addition, the use of AI in national defense, security, and the cyber world could lead to a global AI "arms race." Militarization of AI including development of cyberweapons and "lethal autonomous weapons" (LAWs), which can select and engage human targets without human control, can lead to game-changing military power and regional or global instability. The significant first-mover advantage in militarization of AI disincentivizes actors from taking time for precautions or abiding regulation and standards. Beyond states, "bad actors," including criminals, tyrants, and terrorists, could hack such weapons, initiate cyberattacks using automated AI systems, or develop their own weaponized drones and vehicles to target the public. While policymakers (and AI researchers) in Europe, the United States, and beyond may conceptually agree on the need to ban LAWs, the lack of precise definition on the contours of the notion of militarized AI and lack of global coordination or of the capacity to monitor and enforce decentralized AI development will continue to pose major challenges.

## Approaches to Global Governance of AI

Devising a sustainable and legitimate process to design, agree upon, deploy, and regularly update global governance is key to managing the rise of AI to benefit society. Global governance is needed to shape the competitive landscape to avoid a "race to the bottom" threatening ethical, safety, and human values, while raising standards for beneficial AI innovation. If it is to remain robust and relevant over time, an effective system of AI governance must be anchored in current global governance realities. Furthermore, it must be adaptive to changing power dynamics, especially the growing influence of transnational actors and the private sector.

AI global governance approaches will need to borrow and adapt from other governance regimes including climate change, Internet governance, arms control, international trade, and finance. Government, industry, entrepreneurs, academia, and civil society will all need to be involved in the debate around values, ethical principles, design of international agreements, and their implementation and monitoring.

### *Multi-stakeholder approach to global governance*

Given the global and diverse nature of actors involved in, and affected by, AI development, participation among diverse stakeholders including government, industry, academia, nonprofits, NGOs, and civil society is crucial.

An inclusive multi-stakeholder approach in the discovery, debate, and redefinition around values, ethical principles, design of international agreements, their implementation, and monitoring is likely to raise capacity and buy-in. It also raises legitimacy and credibility among the public.

Given the systemic complexity of the AI revolution, the process should be deeply interdisciplinarity, beyond science, engineering, and business, and actively involve philosophers, artists, sociologists, political scientists, writers, and movie producers. These actors play a key role in shaping governance through their ability to forge the public perception, expectations, and "collective imaginaries" around AI.

### International panel on AI: A way forward?

At this juncture, a legitimate process for establishing consensus among stakeholders regarding the nature, dynamics, impacts, and related challenges in the rise of AI is needed. A relevant example and starting point to develop an inclusive, legitimate process for AI global governance is the Intergovernmental Panel on Climate Change (IPCC). Under the auspices of the United Nations, the IPCC set a widely acknowledged—and yet imperfect—example of a large multi-stakeholder platform driven by science for international consensus building on the pace, dynamics, factors, and consequences of climate change. The IPCC has served as the foundation for designing, implementing, and enforcing global governance and related policies that ultimately culminated in the Paris Agreement under the aegis of the UN.

Like the galaxy of factors and drivers contributing to climate change, AI is a complex phenomenon that is pervasive and distributed across society and the economy. Not attributable to a finite set of producers, it is intertwined with strategic political, trade, and investment interests across states. Given the high systemic complexity, uncertainty, and ambiguity surrounding the rise of AI, its dynamics, and its consequences—a context similar to climate change—creating an IPCC for AI, or "IPAI," can help build a solid base of facts and benchmarks against which to measure progress and inform governance. In terms of the global political objective that AI adoption should serve, there is a growing consensus over the need to position the 17 SDGs—with their subgoals and key performance indicators—as the political compass of the global governance of the AI revolution.

At the beginning of December 2018, Canada and France announced plans to establish an IPAI, modeled on the IPCC. President Emmanuel Macron had proposed the creation of the IPAI while releasing the French AI Strategy in March, ambitiously entitled "AI for Humanity" to signal France's universal aspiration. The IPAI is envisioned as a vessel to inform international dialogue and coordination and pave the way for effective global governance of AI where common ground can be found despite intense competitive dynamics. Like the IPCC, over time the IPAI would gather a large, global, and interdisciplinary group of scientists and experts. It would differ from—and add value to—other existing mechanisms such as the Government Group of Experts (GGE) on Lethal Autonomous Weapon Systems that are held as part of the UN Convention on Certain Conventional Weapons (CCW) as it would be much broader in its mandate and size.

While the IPCC is, by and large, a success story for large-scale multistakeholder governance processes, it is not without its flaws. The IPCC's process of dealing with uncertainties—something that will inevitably plague an IPAI—has been criticized for its lack of precision in its attribution of certainty, ambiguity due to the role value judgments play in assessing its application, and a lack of sensitivity toward political, ethical, and cultural contexts when synthesizing scientific knowledge. In order for an IPAI to garner multilateral governance support, it will need to address these concerns that, at times, stifled effective consensus among such a diverse group of stakeholders, adversely affecting its legitimacy.

Given today's deep and global epistemic crisis, where the authority of science, expertise, information, and representation is being severely questioned, an IPAI will also need to innovate operational processes to achieve more transparency, openness, independence from industry, and inclusion of civil society, without imploding. A concrete area of improvement on IPCC that is aligned with this goal revolves around the level of scrutiny given to the so-called "gray literature" (i.e., non-peer-reviewed or nonpublished in scientific journals) in their assessments. This is particularly crucial in the context of the AI literature: while much of the gray literature includes reports by national academies and legitimate works, there are also articles that engage in fearmongering and popular culture references that generally lack intellectual rigor or scientific merit.

### Strategic mix of "soft" and "hard" law

In addition to an inclusive and legitimate process, global governance approaches will need to deploy a smart and coherent combination of "soft" and "hard" law or governance instruments. Soft law, including industry standards, codes of conduct, norms, and ethical principles, is flexible enough to adapt as technologies as its impacts on society evolve. The Institute of Electrical and Electronics Engineers' (IEEE) Ethically Aligned Design principles is a highly relevant example of industry standards aimed at fostering safe and ethical autonomous and intelligent systems. Hard instruments, such as binding legislation, are also crucial to level the playing field and anchor technological change in a value system. For example, the EU GDPR has created a rigorous legal regime applicable to all organizations that collect, store, process, and circulate personal data of European citizens. Over time, it could mature into a global gold standard law.

In the context of the complex dynamics surrounding the rise of AI, multilateral approaches are needed to level the playing field internationally, raise ethical and safety standards, and orient new technologies toward broad societal benefit. AI is rapidly and significantly transforming societies, and global governance has a central role to play in ensuring its development plays out for good. Innovative and inclusive processes, drawing on a mix of hard and soft instruments, will be key to ensuring that multilateral solutions can rise to the challenge.

## Concluding Remarks

AI is rapidly and significantly transforming societies. However, the rise of AI involves an unprecedented combination of complex dynamics. In this context, global, multi-stakeholder governance to coordinate the rise of AI is necessary to "raise the bar" and shape it toward broad societal benefit. An inclusive international platform such as an International Panel on AI can help build consensus and agreement on the key challenges and concerns in AI. Next, a combination of soft and hard governance and policy modeled on successful examples such as the IEEE and Europe's GDPR exemplify an incremental and pragmatic approach to governance.

## Notes

1   Allan Dafoe. *AI Governance: A Research Agenda* (Oxford: Future of Humanity Institute at the University of Oxford, 2018).
2   McKinsey Global Institute. *Artificial Intelligence, The Next Digital Frontier.* McKinsey and Company, 2017, https://www.mckinsey.com/~/media/McKinsey/Industries/Advanced%20Electronics/Our%20Insights/How%20artificial%20intelligence%20can%20deliver%20real%20value%20to%20companies/MGI-Artificial-Intelligence-Discussion-paper.ashx.
3   Nicolas Miailhe, and Cyrus Hodes. *Making the AI Revolution Work for Everyone—Report to OECD.* The Future Society, AI Initiative, 2017, ai-initiative.org/wp-content/uploads/2017/08/Making-the-AI-Revolution-work-for-everyone.-Report-to-OECD.-MARCH-2017.pdf.
4   Ryan Budish, Herbert Burkert, and Urs Gasser. "Encryption Policy and Its International Impacts: A Framework for Understanding Extraterritorial Ripple Effects." A Hoover Institution Essay, Aegis Series Paper No. 1804, 2018.
5   McKinsey & Company. *Car Data: Paving the Way to Value-Creating Mobility—Perspectives on a New Automotive Business Model,* March 2016. Advanced Industries.

6   PwC. *What Doctor? Why AI and Robotics Will Define New Health*, 2017. https://www.pwc.com/gx/en/news-room/docs/what-doctor-why-ai-and-robotics-will-define-new-health.pdf.

7   Tim Dutton, Brent Barron, and Gaga Boskovic. *Building an AI World: Report on National and Regional AI Strategies*, CIFAR, 2019. https://www.cifar.ca/docs/default-source/ai-society/buildinganaiworld_eng.pdf.

8   Jeffrey Ding. *Deciphering China's AI Dream: The Context, Components, Capabilities, and Consequences of China's Strategy to Lead the World in AI* (Oxford: Future of Humanity Institute at the University of Oxford, 2018).

Chapter 4

# GOVERNMENT 4.0 AND EVIDENCE-BASED POLICIES: AI AND DATA ANALYTICS TO THE RESCUE

Nathalie de Marcellis-Warin and Thierry Warin

## Introduction

Since its origin as a specific field of research in the mid-twentieth century, artificial intelligence (AI) has rapidly evolved (Villani et al., 2018). Designated as a cutting-edge technology, AI can be used in most sectors of our economy, whether manufacturing, finance, transportation, health, or the public sector. In recent years, the discipline has entered a new era, thanks in particular to the development of machine learning (ML), which "includes any information technology that learns and improves from examples, data, and experience, rather than following pre-programmed rules" (Treasury Board of Canada Secretariat, 2019). The digitalization of public administration, the automation of public sector workflows, and policy issues related to this revolution are part of the government transformation toward "Government 4.0."

In this new digital world, the role of governments must be reaffirmed. Within this new technological environment, Government 4.0 has several roles: a facilitator, a user, and a legislator. As a facilitator, the government must support the development and adoption of AI through funding and the creation of entities. It should also help create or promote AI ecosystems. The government must also be a user of AI, using data science and ML techniques in its daily activities, in order to design new public policies. Finally, the government must have a legislative role in several areas, namely ethics, standardization, and privacy.

In this chapter, we will focus on opportunities for governments in the digital age. AI can help them not only in their daily operations but also to solve complex public sector problems. We will present several AI research projects that could help governments in designing or assessing public policies. At the same time, rapid technological changes raise concerns regarding risks and social impacts. We will identify emerging issues and the role of a government as a legislator. It is critical that the use of AI be governed with clear values, ethics, and rules.

## Opportunities of AI and ML for Governments

AI and ML can be used to help the government improve public services and make the best use of its resources. They can also help identify issues in real time that can lead to faster reactions or better decisions. In addition, access to big data—both structured and unstructured data—can help to refine analyses and provide new evidence to build or adapt public policies in this new environment.

### *Improving the government's operational efficiency*

Around governmental agencies, some issues seem to be recurrent, for instance, resource constraints, paperwork burdens, and backlogs. With the application of AI and ML, processing times can be reduced while offering personalized services to citizens and businesses (Benay, 2018).

In several countries, AI technologies are already having an impact on the government's work. The government of Singapore has developed chatbots that can deliver a set of customer services, taking away the need for customers to scroll through numerous pages on the government's websites (Singapore Economic Development Board, 2017). The US Department of Homeland Security's Citizenship and Immigration Services has created a virtual assistant, EMMA, that can respond accurately to human language and answer questions. The Department receives more than 500,000 questions per month. Learning from her own experiences, EMMA gets smarter as she answers more questions. Customers said that its answers have helped (Eggers et al., 2017).

The rise of sophisticated cognitive technologies is aiding advances in several other departments. For instance, speech recognition and machine translation have implications for international relations and the Department of defense. Moreover, computer vision can help to identify thieves by video surveillance. Soon, safety departments will be able to scan license plate numbers of vehicles stopped at red lights, identifying suspects' cars in real time (Eisenberg, 2018). This may also apply for disease surveillance, illustrating a potentially life-saving capability (Eggers et al., 2017). Big data analysis also allows more accurate predictions to be made. The Research Data Archive at the US National Center for Atmospheric Research (NCRA) contains a large and diverse collection of data (meteorological data, oceanographic observations, remote sensing datasets to support atmospheric research, etc.). These multiple sources of big data provide more accurate weather forecasts and, consequently, determine energy production and needs (National Center for Atmospheric Research, 2019).

Revenue and tax agencies also have large volumes of data. Applications based on data science include algorithms that could detect tax evasion. By cross-referencing several data sources, the government can detect whether the reported income actually appears to be what was earned.

Algorithms could also sort through data related to infrastructures to target bridge inspections by cross-referencing with weather data or images taken by drones. Another example is to sift through health and social service data to prioritize cases for child welfare and youth protection (Dhasarathy et al., 2019). These new evidences enable governments to perform more efficiently and generate benefits for the government and citizens.

## *Using data visualization and predictive inference for evidence-based public policies*

All these examples show that governments can effectively use these new technologies to improve public services and save costs. Data science and ML techniques can also be used to help the government in designing new public policies or assess the impact of public policies in place. For some complex issues, there are often large datasets of structured data and unstructured data with hundreds of variables from different sources that are sometimes difficult to compare or use effectively. Data visualization with embedded real-time statistics could help provide a more in-depth analysis of societal issues. Moreover, several policy problems may use predictive modeling. New developments in the field of ML are particularly useful for addressing these prediction problems (Kleinberg et al., 2015). We will present two research projects to illustrate data visualization and the use of ML for public policy.

### *Data visualization and the "FrackMap"*

For some complex issues, several data sources are available, and it is sometimes difficult to use all of them to make an informed decision. Exploration for shale gas in the United States is an example of a complex subject. Whether we look at economic impacts or environmental or human health impacts, it is often difficult to draw an obvious conclusion. To identify and link research on these topics to individual wells and shale plays in the United States, we developed the "FrackMap" (Backus et al., 2019). This map, built on a public domain platform, as a collaboration among the Harvard Chan-NIEHS Center for Environmental Health, the UPENN Center of Excellence in Environmental Toxicology, the Harvard Center for Geographic Analysis, and the data science platform nüance-R, shows the geospatial association of *research articles* to *individual wells, shales, or regions of unconventional drilling* as well as *geolocated Tweets* talking about shale gas and fracking.

Based on the latest developments in data science, we coded algorithms to perform some text analysis of tweets related to fracking. The FrackMap is truly a unique and useful tool for the public health policymakers. They can infer correlations between various layers of the map (for instance, the number of wells and the number of publications related to health impacts in the same area). The temporal and spatial information embedded in tweets can also be used to contextualize the layer dedicated to the scientific research analysis, which helps improve public understanding of environmental and human health impacts, inform public policy, and support health policies and environmental justice. This tool can also contribute to the formulation of energy policies with low impact on health, the environment, and the climate.

*ML to predict the migration flow process in China*

Advances in computer science combined with a recognition of its applicability to economic and public policy questions make it a new tool for economists. Usually, econometric models cull the immense proliferation of explanatory variables into a tractable and parsimonious list. However, there are several problems with this approach that in turn hint at fundamental gaps in our understanding of societal changes. An ML framework can precisely fill these kinds of gaps in evidence and improve prediction for public policies.

Bengoa and Warin (2019) have developed an ML framework to predict health issues for internal migrants in China (Hukou system). In such a framework, different algorithms are trained to identify an internally validated set of correlates. ML helps to find causality instead of correlations. Why does it matter for public policies? Causality means one variable is identified prior to other significant factors. This matters a lot for public policies since officials can now target the first indicator instead of looking at a portfolio of potential indicators. Public policies may gain in terms of efficiency as well as costs.

There are not many studies that have addressed this link between migration with limited access to healthcare and health outcomes in developing economies. Other studies suggest that migrants are reasonably healthy at the point of migration but more likely to experience adverse effects than nonmigrants. As they get injured and do not have access to health some return home while others remain in urban areas. The existing Hukou household registration system imposes restrictions and limits on where to live, which is determined mainly by birth. Hukou card is an internal passport that gives access to education and health services. Bengoa and Warin (2019) have showed that China's Hukou reform is a move in the right direction. Pilot programs in 29 provinces are helping to raise awareness about the necessity to eliminate barriers to health access, which are now linked to geography. In 2015, Shanghai had approximately 9.8 million migrant workers holding a rural Hukou.

## Challenges for Governments in Implementing AI

However, the government must overcome some obstacles if it wants to benefit from AI solutions. First, the public sector continues to be plagued by an aging information technology (IT) infrastructure. Another difficulty faced in transforming the government to use AI and ML is the lack of statistical awareness and tool experience throughout the ranks of analysts (Eisenberg, 2018). In addition to these issues, similar to those of large nontechnology companies, structural issues must be addressed if the government is to legitimately position itself as a user of AI solutions (Gouvernement du Québec, 2018). The essential condition for the use of AI by governments is the accessibility of public data and at the same time the protection of personal data and their ethical use.

### *The difficulty of accessing (good-quality) data*

The *Open Data Barometer* assesses the openness of government data in key sectors, including education, health, the environment, and public expenditure. The latest edition suggests that most government datasets are still not open (World Wide Web Foundation, 2018). Moreover, agency-specific IT and data governance protocols are often misaligned. This lack of interoperability limits how agencies can integrate multiple databases that ML algorithms can then analyze and use to provide richer insights (Desouza, 2018).

This question is indeed decisive, since application development in this field requires massive amounts of data. Many countries are considering in their AI strategies making better use of the government's asset to support business access to the data required to build successful applications. Finland makes the openness and use of data collected by Finnish ministries and agencies a priority (Gouvernement du Québec, 2018). Government agencies would sometimes wish to make public data available to research centers, start-ups, and companies to develop products and services that can benefit society as a whole, but this cannot be done without adequate consideration of citizens' rights (Gouvernement du Québec, 2018).

Data can be incomplete, biased, and of poor quality. AI techniques require high-quality data, otherwise they may lead to discriminatory outcomes or have other undesired effects. Governments should value more of their data as well as improve their data quality. To go further, governments that use algorithms and AI systems for public policies may want to open up the data used in the policy-making process (World Wide Web Foundation, 2018). The management and circulation of these data require certain conditions (e.g., anonymization and exclusive use for training new models), which would be established not only by the participating organizations but also by the people to whom the data relate (e.g., public transportation or taxi users, hospital or clinic patients). There are ways to overcome this major obstacle. For example, countries such as the United Kingdom have considered creating data trusts to ensure a better dissemination and exploitation of data (Gouvernement du Québec, 2018).

The government must adopt best practices in its ability to open up its data to promote their best use for the benefit of the community, which will be beneficial for the development of new AI applications by and for the country. This access to data in no way constitutes a disempowerment of the government with regard to the need to protect privacy. However, this responsibility must now be balanced with the responsibility to deploy and enhance data for the common good (Gouvernement du Québec, 2018). At the European level, several ongoing reforms are expected to improve access and data flows. Villani et al. (2018) suggested that the public authorities must initiate new modes of production, collaboration, and governance of data, through the creation of "data commons." The government can play a role as a trusted third party.

### Ethics, standardization, and privacy

The government must have the role of legislator in several areas of ethics, standardization, and privacy. Governments need to also ensure that their policies and regulations are coherent with AI evolution (Bharadwaj, 2019).

Indeed, open data come with the modernization of the regulations surrounding the use of public data. For instance, in Quebec (Canada), the government needs to modernize the *Act respecting access to documents held by public bodies and the protection of personal information (chapter A-2.1)*. This is not only to enable the adoption of AI within government but also to give the ecosystem the opportunity to value anonymized public data in their own application development. Obviously, a rigorous but agile mechanism will have to be put in place to avoid slippage and leakage of sensitive information.

According to the CIRANO Barometer 2018, an annual survey of the Quebec population on the level of risk perception related to 47 social issues,

47 percent of Quebecers are concerned with the protection of personal data collected by connected objects and AI and 34 percent of Quebecers want the government to provide an ethical framework for the development of AI (De Marcellis-Warin and Peignier, 2018).

Transparency and ethical uses of data become critical issues with the move toward AI, increasing the need to develop new ethical frameworks around algorithms that support decision-making. Public agencies need to educate people about these systems, be transparent in their design, and make clear how to deduce and report errors. The development of predictive algorithms can also result in biases based on gender or race, not because they are designed with biases in mind but because they may learn from data that are not representative of the population.

It will be important to have frameworks in place to review and check cognitive systems, to safeguard against these issues (Desouza, 2018). "It will become increasingly important to develop AI algorithms that are not just powerful and scalable, but also transparent to inspection, predictable, robust against manipulation and able to find the person responsible" (Bostrom and Yudkowsky, 2014).

Several initiatives have been launched around the world, in particular the *Montreal Declaration for Responsible AI* in 2017 (Montreal Declaration for Responsible AI, 2018). The Declaration has three main objectives: develop an ethical framework for the development and deployment of AI, guide the digital transition so that everyone benefits from this technological revolution, and open a national and international forum for discussion to collectively achieve equitable, inclusive, and ecologically sustainable AI development. The *Montreal Declaration* concerns any person or organization willing to promote the responsible development of AI, "whether it is to contribute scientifically or technologically, to develop social projects, to elaborate rules (regulations, codes) that apply to it, to be able to contest bad or unwise approaches, or to be able to alert public opinion when necessary" (Montreal Declaration for Responsible AI, 2018). It is also useful for political representatives, whether elected or named, whose citizens expect them to take stock of developing social changes, quickly establish a framework allowing a digital transition that serves the greater good, and anticipate the serious risks presented by the development of AI applications.

Public agencies, and especially agencies that have specific audit and inspection mandates, need to develop capabilities to audit and inspect AI systems. Given that these systems do not have agreed-upon models and step-by-step functions that can be audited, innovations in auditing are required (Desouza, 2018). The creation of specific norms and standards for AI has intensified in recent years. In 2017, ISO set up Subcommittee 42 to centralize and initiate the activities of the IT standardization program in the field of AI (Gouvernement du Québec, 2018). Governments can seek out academic institutions in their communities to work on AI development initiatives. Academic partners are often a rich source of specialized knowledge in a domain and can bring the necessary computational and analytical knowledge to bear (Desouza, 2018).

## Conclusion

AI-based programs can help governments cut costs and save labor hours, which can be then used for more complex tasks and deliver faster services. AI systems can also play a role in increasing objectivity for decision-making. To the extent that biases may play a role in deciding court sentencing for instance, AI systems can be deployed jointly with humans so as to analyze the results of decisions and use this data to identify any anomalies (Desouza, 2018). Government 4.0 should be an "AI-augmented government" (Eggers et al., 2017). This means that governments should build and increase their capacity to use as well as govern AI (Brundage and Bryson, 2016). For that, governments must enhance their expertise through policy changes that will support multidisciplinary talent development.

## Acknowledgments

The authors would like to thank CIRANO for its support and more specifically Marine Leroi, research professional at CIRANO. The usual caveats apply.

## References

Backus, Ann, Nathalie De Marcellis-Warin, and Thierry Warin. 2019. "Shale Gas Extraction in the United States: Perspectives from Geo-Located Twitter Conversations and Academic Publications." American Economic Association Annual meeting, Session: Artificial Intelligence, Data Science and Economics at the Crossroads, January 5, 2019. doi:10.6084/m9.figshare.8847842.v1.

Benay, Alex. 2018. "Using Artificial Intelligence in Government Means Balancing Innovation with the Ethical and Responsible Use of Emerging Technologies." June 18, 2019, https://open.canada.ca/en/blog/using-artificial-intelligence-government-means-balancing-innovation-ethical-and-responsible.

Bengoa, Marta, and Thierry Warin. 2019. "Hukou System, Access to Health Services and Health Outcomes: A Machine Learning Approach Applied to Rural-Urban Migration in China." American Economic Association Annual meeting, Session: Artificial Intelligence, Data Science and Economics at the Crossroads, January 5, 2019. doi: 10.6084/m9.figshare.8847860.v1.

Bharadwaj, Raghav. 2019. "AI in Government—Current AI Projects in the Public Sector." Emerj, May 3, 2019, https://emerj.com/ai-sector-overviews/ai-government-current-ai-projects-public-sector/.

Bostrom, Nick and Eliezer Yudkowsky, 2014. "The ethics of artificial intelligence". In K. Frankish and W. Ramsey (Eds.), *The Cambridge Handbook of Artificial Intelligence* (pp. 316–334). Cambridge: Cambridge University Press. doi:10.1017/CBO9781139046855.020.

Brundage, Miles, and Joanna Bryson. 2016. "Smart Policies for Artificial Intelligence." June 9, 2019, *ArXiv:1608.08196 [Cs]*, August, https://arxiv.org/abs/1608.08196.

De Marcellis-Warin, Nathalie, and Ingrid Peignier. 2018. *Perception Des Risques Au Québec, Baromètre CIRANO 2018.* https://doi.org/10.6084/m9.figshare.7575584.

Desouza, Kevin C. 2018. "Delivering Artificial Intelligence in Government: Challenges and Opportunities." December 13, 2018, http://www.businessofgovernment.org/sites/default/files/Delivering%20Artificial%20Intelligence%20in%20Government.pdf.

Dhasarathy, Anusha, Sahil Jain and Naufal Khan, 2019. *When governments turn to AI: Algorithms, trade-offs, and trust.* McKinsey. February.

Eggers, William D., David Schatsky, and Peter Viechnicki. 2017. "AI-Augmented Government: Using Cognitive Technologies to Redesign Public Sector Work." May 3, 2019, https://www2.deloitte.com/insights/us/en/focus/cognitive-technologies/artificial-intelligence-government.html.

Eisenberg, Samuel. 2018. "Chapter 3—Machine Learning for the Government: Challenges and Statistical Difficulties." In *Federal Data Science*, edited by Feras A. Batarseh and Ruixin Yang, 29–40. Academic Press, Elsevier, Cambridge, MA. doi:10.1016/B978-0-12-812443-7.00003-X.

Gouvernement du Québec. 2018. "Stratégie Pour l'essor de l'écosystème Québécois En Intelligence Artificielle", Rapport du Comité d'orientation de la grappe en intelligence artificielle remis au Ministère de l'économie, de la science et de l'innovation. 93 pages. https://ia.quebec/wp-content/uploads/2018/06/Strategie-IA-vDEF-19-juin-2018-v8.pdf (Last access on July 14, 2020).

Kleinberg, Jon, Jens Ludwig, Sendhil Mullainathan, and Ziad Obermeyer. 2015. "Prediction Policy Problems." *American Economic Review*, 105 (5): 491–95. doi:10.1257/aer.p20151023.

Montreal Declaration for Responsible AI. 2018. "Montreal Declaration for a Responsible Development of Artificial Intelligence 2018." June 18, 2019, https://www.montrealdeclaration-responsibleai.com/the-declaration.

National Center for Atmospheric Research. 2019. "NCAR's RDA." https://rda.ucar.edu/#!about.

Singapore Economic Development Board. 2017. "Why Singapore Has Become a Thriving Hub for AI." December 13, 2018, https://www.edb.gov.sg/en/news-and-events/insights/innovation/why-singapore-has-become-a-thriving-hub-for-ai.html.

Treasury Board of Canada Secretariat. 2019. "Directive on Automated Decision-Making." June 9, 2019, https://www.tbs-sct.gc.ca/pol/doc-eng.aspx?id=32592&section=html.

Villani, Cédric, Yann Bonnet, Charly Berthet, François Levin, Marc Schoenauer, Anne Charlotte Cornut, and Bertrand Rondepierre. 2018. *Donner un sens à l'intelligence artificielle: pour une stratégie nationale et européenne.* Conseil national du numérique.

World Wide Web Foundation. 2018. "How Open Data Can Save AI." June 18, 2019, https://webfoundation.org/2018/01/how-open-data-can-save-ai/.

# Chapter 5

# THE STRATEGIC IMPLICATIONS OF ARTIFICIAL INTELLIGENCE FOR INTERNATIONAL SECURITY

## Jean-Marc Rickli

Artificial intelligence (AI) has profound consequences for any human activity including those that involve the use of force and violence. This chapter looks at the strategic implications of AI for international security. To that purpose it first analyzes the economic implications of AI for jobs creation and destruction and their impact on social stability. It then looks at how AI empowers individuals to a level unseen before in international security. To illustrate this, the chapter considers how individuals can use AI to manipulate written, visual, audio content to create fake news and alternative realities. Finally, the chapter talks about the growing autonomy in weapons systems and the challenges this represents for international stability.

## The Economic Strategic Implications of AI

Although there is no consensus among analysts on the impact of AI for the global economy, two assumptions seem to be shared: that productivity will increase and that AI will lead to profound transformations of employment with the destruction of traditional jobs and the creation of new ones. The balance of these transformations, however, is unknown and left to various speculations.

A study by Accenture estimates that AI technologies could boost labor productivity by up to 40 percent in 2035.[1] A research by Pricewaterhouse Coopers (PWC) estimates that AI could add $15.7 trillion to global GDP by 2030, an increase of 14 percent from now.[2] For McKinsey & Company, global GDP

The author would like to thank Alexander Jahns and Olivier Delage for the research conducted for this chapter could be boosted by about 1.2 percent a year.[3] For this strategic consulting company this implies that "AI is moving from the lab to the workplace, with profound implications for business and society."[4] Accenture finds that AI has the potential to double the annual economic growth rates of 12 developed economies.[5] The rate of AI adoption and integration in the economy has, however, the potential to increase the digital divide between advanced and developing economies. The gap between these countries in terms of net GDP impact could widen from "three percentage points in 2025 to 19 percentage points in 2030," increasing further the development gap worldwide.[6]

The potential that AI has in automating many of the tasks undertaken by humans across a range of sectors also has a silver lining. While providing businesses with increasingly larger profit margins, automation will have a serious impact on the labor market by provoking profound changes in the employment structure and likely lead to the rise of social inequality. It is indeed predicted that many jobs, especially at the bottom of the chain, will disappear. McKinsey estimates that around 50 percent of current work activities are technically automatable by adapting currently demonstrated technologies.[7] Similarly, the consulting company estimates that 78 percent of "predicable physical work" can feasibly be automated (assembly line, food preparation, soldering) while 25 percent of unpredictable physical work could be automated (such as construction or forestry).[8] In the end, McKinsey estimates that up to 800 million jobs could be displaced by 2030 worldwide due to automation.[9]

Job profiles that are "characterized by repetitive tasks and activities that require low digital skills may experience the largest decline as a share of total employment, from some 40 percent to near 30 percent by 2030" and that in return, jobs that involve "nonrepetitive activities and those that require high digital skills" can rise from "40 percent to more than 50 percent by 2030."[10] One such example could be the automotive and transport industry. With the ever-growing sophistication and availability of self-driving cars and drones, one can easily imagine that industrial transportation will become increasingly automated. This would lead to the disappearance of jobs on a large scale. In economy, if one considers that 10 percent of global unemployment represents a major recession, and 20 percent a global emergency, then the figures from various studies, where up to 15 percent of the global workforce will have to change their employment—and some will not manage the transition—make the digital revolution supported by AI a period with profound socioeconomic consequences.[11]

Some do argue that jobs will simply migrate and that AI will ultimately create more jobs than will be lost.[12] Independently from whether this will come true or not, society will still have to manage an initial loss of jobs in many sectors, before entire workforces from different industries migrate to entirely new lines of work. This includes training for changing occupation, learning how to work in tandem with a machine, and learning new skills to thrive in the workplace.[13] This will imply a lot of re- and upskilling that will most probably leave many people on the wayside.

The most significant national actors in the development of AI are the United States and China. According to a study by CB Insights in 2018, American companies dominate the global landscape of privatized investment for AI, with 76 of the top 100 companies located in the United States as compared to only 6 in China.[14] A report by EconSight suggests that Microsoft leads the industry in innovation because it has filed 20 percent of the "world-class patents" out of the top 30 companies in the field.[15] However, IBM has the largest total AI patent portfolio with approximately 8,290 applications.[16] In aggregate, US companies have led the international community in AI patents since 2010, with 79,936 of the more than 154,000 AI patents filed world-wide originating in the United States during that time period.[17] However, China is starting to narrow the patent gap and the World Intellectual Property Organization reports that China is now producing more patents each year than the United States.[18] Similarly, China also produces a majority of the research papers published on AI. In 2018, a total of 27,321 research papers were Chinese as compared to only 23,965 in the United States.[19]

As both countries have recognized that AI will be a key enabler of not only their economic development but more importantly of their strategy for global reach, it is very likely that the twenty-first century will be marked by a strong geopolitical rivalry between China and the United States. The current crisis around Huawei is an early illustration of this dynamics. The competition for AI dominance will be a key characteristic of this race for global power. Thus, the 13th Chinese 5-Year Plan (2016–20) includes a variety of initiatives aimed at getting China to technological parity with Western industrialized countries, including the Made in China 2025 Plan, the Robotics Industry Development Plan (2016–20), and the State Council Notice on Issuing the Action Outline for Promoting the Development of Big Data.[20] On July 20, 2018, the Chinese State Council released the "New Generation of Artificial Intelligence Development Plan," which presents a detailed plan of China's global AI aspirations. Partly as a response to China's ambitious policy in AI, President Trump issued an Executive Order on "Maintaining American Leadership in Artificial Intelligence in February 2019."[21] Similarly, the US Defense Advanced Research Program Agency (DARPA) also announced a $2 billion campaign to develop the next generation of AI technologies for national security purposes.[22]

The changes prompted by AI will also profoundly challenge domestic and international governance systems as unlike the Industrial Revolution that took more than a hundred years to unfold, the current transformations driven by emerging technologies and notably AI and known under the term of the

Fourth Industrial Revolution are extremely rapid due to the phenomenal rate of digital diffusion. The latter is mainly driven by the private sector and the world's largest technology companies such as the American GAFAM and NATU and the Chinese BATX,[23] which acquire increasing influence toward states.[24] Thus, when Apple became the first ever company to reach a market valuation of $1 trillion in August 2018, its worth was more than 1 percent of the world's GDP (estimated at $80.6 trillion) and larger than the GDP of each of the 184 out of the 200 countries listed in the 2017 World Bank database.[25] This is remarkable and promises to profoundly transform global politics as nonstate actors such as the big multinational digital companies can nowadays wield economic power that most states are unable to match. Even developed states are affected by the competition with the big tech firms. For instance, Britain now faces a brain drain in AI from its top universities to the tech firms of Silicon Valley.[26]

## The Empowerment of Individuals by AI

Beyond fueling great power rivalries, AI diffuses power not only to transnational actors such as multinational companies, as noted previously, but also to individuals and nonstate actors. The rapid proliferation of AI to individuals is due to its exponential growth as well as its dual-use nature. AI recent breakthroughs have been achieved by the combination of increasing computing power and the phenomenal creation of data in our increasing digitalized world. This trend is magnified with the advent of the Internet of Things (IoT).

In computer science, Moore's law indicates that the processing power of computers doubles every 18 months. In 2018, it was found that the amount of computer used in the largest AI training runs doubled every 3.5 months from 2012 to 2018. This represents a more than 300,000 times increase compared to a twelve times increase based on Moore's law for the same period. These exponential computing capabilities are fueled by a similar growth in data generation. With the rise of IoT the increasing number of computers and connected devices generates an explosion of data. It is estimated that 23.14 billion connected devices were in use worldwide in 2018 and 30.73 billion will be by the end of 2020.[27] These will generate 44 zettabytes of data,[28] or the equivalent of 5,200 gigabytes for every individual. The latter represent more than half of the printed collection of the entire Library of Congress.[29]

The fact that AI is a dual-use technology, that as shown in the previous section it is primarily developed in the private sector, and that it develops at an exponential rate provides individuals with an unparalleled access to wield power in human history. Nowadays, with emerging technologies and the digitalization of the world, each individual can potentially have a strategic impact. One just has to think about the amount of data stolen by Edward Snowden or Bradley Manning (hundreds of thousands to a few million documents) to realize that no spy could ever have realized this feat until very recently without the digital revolution.[30] The latter is one of the necessary conditions for AI to thrive.

The proliferation of AI is also due to a drop in its costs due to rapid technological developments in machine learning and other algorithmic techniques as well as the fact that algorithms increasingly rely on open-source developments.[31] As a consequence of these costs shifts, "lower barriers to entry incentivizes new actors to search for opportunities to exploit security for economic or political gain."[32] This is even more true in the cyber domain, where the acquisition of new cyber capabilities is cheap, and the marginal cost of additional production—adding a target—is almost zero.[33] It follows that the increasing automation of tasks imply that existing actors can potentially become more dangerous because it increases the reach and scalability of their misdeeds.

An early example of how AI can be misused and spread very quickly is deepfakes. Deepfakes are AI-forged images and videos that enable the recreation of the facial and vocal features of a person, with uncanny accuracy.[34] Deepfakes are created through a technique called generative adversarial networks or GANs. GANs rely on the application of game theory to algorithms. Two neural networks, a generator and a discriminator, are pitted against each other in a zero-sum game scenario. In this scenario, the generator produces images that the discriminator rates by telling the generator the differences between the fake and real images. The generators and the discriminator are both getting very rapidly better at producing fake pictures and conversely at spotting fake ones.[35]

This technique was invented in 2014 but the first deepfake videos appeared at the end of 2017. In December 2017, the first face-swap porn video was created. Less than two months later, an application called FakeApp that allowed anyone to recreate face-swap porn videos with their own datasets was launched.[36] Since then, GANs have been used to fake pictures, videos, and voices. Baidu even claims that it only needs 3.7 seconds of audio of a voice to reproduce it.[37]

Misuses of this technique have proliferated accordingly. Thus, GANs have been used to fake satellite pictures,[38] create fake UN speeches,[39] or hack MRI pictures.[40] The most recent deepfake application, DeepNude, was created to remove clothing from the images of any woman, making them realistically nude. The app developer used an open-source algorithm developed by the University of California, Berkeley, to create DeepNude.[41] Though the developer rapidly took down this application, this examples demonstrates how AI is providing any individual with tools of massive manipulation. The consequent democratization of voice and image forgery tools and techniques enabled by AI contributes to eroding trust by making any piece of media on the Internet suspicious. For Kissinger, this prompts the "end of truth," which is leading to the "end of the Enlightenment era."[42]

## The Militarization of AI

The transformative nature of AI has also military applications and implications. The nature of violence and warfare is indeed evolving, with states and nonstate actors increasingly relying on both human and technological surrogates to use force in the twenty-first century.[43] When it comes to technological surrogates, the increasing autonomy of machines and robots afforded by AI represents the new silver bullet of future conflicts. In 2016, the Defense Science Board of the US Department of Defense released its first study on autonomy. The report concluded that the US DoD "must take immediate action to accelerate its exploitation of autonomy while also preparing to counter autonomy employed by adversaries. [...] Rapid transition of autonomy into warfighting capabilities is vital if the U.S. is to sustain military advantage."[44] This launched a global competition for AI supremacy among the great powers (China, Russia, and the United States) as well as regional actors such as Israel.

The militarization of AI as well as the repurpose of its original use also expand existing threats, introduce new ones as AI systems can complete tasks more successfully, and alter the typical character of threats, making attacks typically more effective, more finely targeted, more difficult to attribute, and more likely to exploit vulnerabilities in other AI systems.[45] Due to the scalability, efficiency, and ease of diffusion of AI systems, the cost (in terms of resources, manpower, and psychological distance) of carrying out attacks will be lower, increasing the number of malevolent actors as well as the number of attacks that can be carried out.[46]

The militarization of AI is also very likely to have a direct impact on strategic stability as it will affect the balance between the offensive and the defensive. Strategic stability refers to the absence of incentives to attack first. Nowadays, it usually refers to the absence of incentives to use nuclear weapons first (in preemptive attacks) and the absence of incentives to build up those forces.[47] Hence the issue of AI on nuclear strategy and deterrence is of utmost importance for the future of international security.

The emerging literature dealing with AI and nuclear risk adopts contrasted views about the dangers posed by AI for nuclear stability. For some, machine learning and automation concerning nuclear command-and-control ($C^2$) systems can bring some "qualitative improvements" as well as "make nuclear delivery systems capable of navigating to their target more autonomously and precisely."[48] Michael C. Horowitz raises interesting points concerning potential qualitative improvements brought by the introduction of autonomous systems into the $C^2$ architecture but he mentions that it is necessary to consider the fact that there are still "potential risks due to the potential for automation bias, even if there is still a human in the chain of command."[49] With regard to nuclear delivery platforms, Horowitz also argues that an autonomous nuclear delivery platform (e.g., combat aircraft, bomber, or submarine) will still be vulnerable to "hacking or spoofing."[50] These kinds of risks could lead to probable nuclear crises and therefore put nuclear strategic stability in danger.

However, considering the ethos of traditional military that relies on the predictability of the weapons behavior, especially when it comes to nuclear weapons, it is very unlikely that autonomous nuclear weapons will be developed. Hence, the major destabilizing factors that could trigger a nuclear escalation would probably not come from atomic weapons but from conventional military uses of AI that "could place pressure on nuclear powers to adopt unstable launch postures or even to strike first in a crisis."[51] The reasons are several but have to do with the increasing tempo of operations that AI will lead to in military operations,[52] the misperception of the adversary's AI capacities,[53] as well as the risks that corrupted data analyzed by AI could lead to "catastrophic reactions, including escalation and retaliation."[54]

As the nature of AI is digital, similar problems in applying deterrence theory to the cyber domain emerge in the conflict dynamics prodded by AI. Taddeo rightly observes that if the instigators as well as the damages of cyberattacks cannot be fully identified, "it is impossible to issue a meaningful threat" of retaliation. This could also lead to a risk of overreaction. Moreover, unlike nuclear deterrence which relies on a clear messaging of the nuclear capabilities, deterrence in the cyber domain relies on noncommunication. Indeed, if a "cyberweapon is actually demonstrated, then the enemy may create a remedy and the offender would lose superiority."[55] These issues are therefore making the strategic environment of cybersecurity one of persistent offence, where taking offensive actions is tactically and strategically more advantageous than taking defensive ones. Similar problems of deterrence will apply with AI especially when it comes to the use of AI in the cyber domain.

Although we have not yet seen autonomous cyber weapons, IBM has developed a proof of concept of an AI-powered malware. It is "highly targeted and evasive" because unlike traditional malware, it hides its malicious payload in a benign carrier application such as a video application and uses AI to create unique trigger conditions that can only be unlocked if the intended target is identified.[56] A neural network is indeed trained to recognize the target, for instance, a person, that will trigger the attack once identified.

This type of attack opens the possibility for hyper discriminate attacks that can be reproduced easily by training neural networks to identify new targets. The use of AI in the cyber domain will also improve infiltration by "autonomous agents capable of 'remembering' the information gathered during reconnaissance and using it to plan an infiltration path." This could also be used in combination with big data analysis in order to strike the most vulnerable infrastructure, "or choose the best timing to make an attack most catastrophic."[57] AI will also facilitate and improve the use of malware acting as swarms that are "sets of decentralised, cooperating autonomous agents that can form a whole new kind of botnet, where there is no need for a centralised command and control."[58]

In the physical battlefield, the weaponization of AI will also allow the development of swarming strategies. Swarming combines the military principles of mass, coordination, speed, and concentration of forces at new levels. Autonomous swarms will allow the concentration of large numbers of military assets with very few or no human controllers and with far quicker reaction times to constantly changing situations. The use of swarms will saturate the adversary's defense system by synchronizing a series of simultaneous and concentrated attacks.[59] Some posit that the development of autonomous weapons systems and the proliferation of their use in swarms will probably have a destabilizing impact on strategic stability in the future through the neutralization of adversary's defense systems, thereby giving an advantage to the offensive.[60]

Overall, the weaponization of AI will challenge deterrence and strategic stability. If deterrence is no longer feasible, then it is very likely that it will be replaced by preemption, a very unstable international configuration that encourages escalation and arms races.[61] Preemption represents also a violation of article 2(4) of the UN Charter as it implies attacking before being attacked.[62] Thus, full autonomy in weapons system has the potential to completely upset international strategic stability as well as international law.[63]

## Conclusions

AI will alter international security by rebalancing the international balance of power, empowering individuals, and shifting the global strategic balance. The weaponization of AI will also challenge the concept of nuclear deterrence.[64] Two states, China and the United States, are currently dominating the AI market with innovations in both the economic and military domains. Beyond fueling great power rivalries, AI also potentially diffuses power to transnational actors such as multinational companies as well as individuals and nonstate actors. The dual-use nature of AI enables a very fast proliferation of its applications that empowers individuals and nonstate actors who can find ways to leverage this technology. Overall, the proliferation of AI and its potential misuse, malicious use, and weaponization can profoundly alter the nature of international security by shifting the referent of international security from 195 states to potentially more than 7.5 billion individuals that could all potentially become sources of international insecurity if they manage to leverage the power unleashed by AI and use it in malicious ways.[65]

## Notes

1  Marc Purdy and Paul Daugherty. *Why Artificial Intelligence Is the Future of Growth*, Accenture, 2016, p. 17, https://www.accenture.com/t00010101T000000__w__/gb-en/_acnmedia/PDF-33/Accenture-Why-AI-is-the-Future-of-Growth.PDF#zoom=50.
2  Nicolas Rapp and Brian O'Keefe. "These 100 Companies Are Leading the Way in AI," *Fortune*, January 8, 2018, http://fortune.com/2018/01/08/artificial-intelligence-ai-companies-invest-startups/.
3  Jacques Bughin, Jeongmin Seong, James Manyika, Michael Chui and Raoul Joshi. *Notes from the AI Frontier: Modelling the Impact of AI on the World Economy*, McKinsey Global Institute, September 2018, p. 3, https://www.mckinsey.com/featured-insights/artificial-intelligence/notes-from-the-ai-frontier-modeling-the-impact-of-ai-on-the-world-economy.
4  McKinsey Insights. "Artificial Intelligence," *McKinsey & Company*, 2019, https://www.mckinsey.com/featured-insights/artificial-intelligence.
5  PricewaterhouseCoopers. *Sizing the Price: What's the Real Value of AI for Your Business and How Can You Capitalise*, PwC, 2017, https://www.pwc.com/gx/en/issues/analytics/assets/pwc-ai-analysis-sizing-the-prize-report.pdf, and Marc Purdy and Paul Daugherty. *Why Artificial Intelligence Is the Future of Growth*. Accenture, 2016, p. 3, https://www.accenture.com/t00010101T000000__w__/gb-en/_acnmedia/PDF-33/Accenture-Why-AI-is-the-Future-of-Growth.PDF#zoom=50.
6  Jacques Bughin, Jeongmin Seong, James Manyika, Michael Chui and Raoul Joshi. *Notes from the AI Frontier: Modelling the Impact of AI on the World Economy*, McKinsey Global Institute, September 2018, p. 34, https://www.mckinsey.com/featured-insights/artificial-intelligence/notes-from-the-ai-frontier-modeling-the-impact-of-ai-on-the-world-economy.
7  James Manyika and Keving Sneader. "AI, Automation and the Future of Work: Ten Things to Solve for," *Mckinsey*, June 2018, https://www.mckinsey.com/featured-insights/future-of-work/ai-automation-and-the-future-of-work-ten-things-to-solve-for.
8  Julia Bossmann. "Top 9 Ethical Issues in Artificial Intelligence," *World Economic Forum*, October 21, 2016, https://www.weforum.org/agenda/2016/10/top-10-ethical-issues-in-artificial-intelligence/.
9  Jacques Bughin, Susan Lund, Michael Chui, Jacques Bughin, Jonathan Woetzel, Parul Batra, Ryan Ko and Saurabh Sanghvi . *Jobs Lost, Jobs Gained: Workforce Transition in a Time of Automation*, McKinsey Global Institute, December 2017, p. 11, https://www.mckinsey.com/~/media/mckinsey/featured%20insights/future%20of%20organizations/what%20the%20future%20of%20work%20will%20mean%20for%20jobs%20skills%20and%20wages/mgi%20jobs%20lost-jobs%20gained_report_december%202017.ashx.

10   Jacques Bughin, Jeongmin Seong, James Manyika, Michael Chui and Raoul Joshi. *Notes from the AI Frontier: Modelling the Impact of AI on the World Economy*, McKinsey Global Institute, September 2018, p. 4, https://www.mckinsey.com/featured-insights/artificial-intelligence/notes-from-the-ai-frontier-modeling-the-impact-of-ai-on-the-world-economy.

11   James Manyika, Susan Lund, Michael Chui, Jacques Bughin, Jonathan Woetzel, Parul Batra, Ryan Ko and Saurabh Sanghvi. *Jobs Lost, Jobs Gained: Workforce Transition in a Time of Automation*, McKinsey Global Institute, December 2017, p. 1, https://www.mckinsey.com/~/media/mckinsey/featured%20insights/future%20of%20organizations/what%20the%20future%20of%20work%20will%20mean%20for%20jobs%20skills%20and%20wages/mgi%20jobs%20lost-jobs%20gained_report_december%202017.ashx.

12   James Manyika and Kevin Sneader. "AI, Automation and the Future of Work: Ten Things to Solve for," *McKinsey*, June 2018, https://www.mckinsey.com/featured-insights/future-of-work/ai-automation-and-the-future-of-work-ten-things-to-solve-for.

13   James Manyika and Kevin Sneader. "AI, Automation and the Future of Work: Ten Things to Solve for," *McKinsey*, June 2018, https://www.mckinsey.com/featured-insights/future-of-work/ai-automation-and-the-future-of-work-ten-things-to-solve-for.

14   CB Insights. "AI 100: The Artificial Intelligence Startups Redefining Industries," *CB insights*, February 6, 2019, https://www.cbinsights.com/research/artificial-intelligence-top-startups/.

15   Louis Columbus. "Microsoft Leads the AI Patent Race Going into 2019," *Forbes*, January 6, 2019, https://www.forbes.com/sites/louiscolumbus/2019/01/06/microsoft-leads-the-ai-patent-race-going-into-2019/#21d7852144de.

16   WIPO. *WIPO Technology Trends 2019: Artificial Intelligence*. Geneva: World Intellectual Property Organization, 2019, https://www.wipo.int/edocs/pubdocs/en/wipo_pub_1055.pdf.

17   Louis Columbus. "Microsoft Leads the AI Patent Race Going into 2019," *Forbes*, January 6, 2019, https://www.forbes.com/sites/louiscolumbus/2019/01/06/microsoft-leads-the-ai-patent-race-going-into-2019/#21d7852144de.

18   WIPO. *WIPO Technology Trends 2019: Artificial Intelligence*. Geneva: World Intellectual Property Organization, 2019, https://www.wipo.int/edocs/pubdocs/en/wipo_pub_1055.pdf.

19   Tom Simonite. "China Is Catching Up to the US in AI Research—Fast," *Wired*, March 13, 2019, https://www.wired.com/story/china-catching-up-us-in-ai-research/.

20   Tsinghua University. "China AI Development Report," *China Institute for Science and Technology Policy at Tsinghua University*, 2018, http://www.sppm.tsinghua.edu.cn/eWebEditor/UploadFile/China_AI_development_report_2018.pdf.

21   Exec. Order No. 13,859, 3 C.F.R. 3967–3972 (2019), https://www.whitehouse.gov/presidential-actions/executive-order-maintaining-american-leadership-artificial-intelligence/.

22   John Villasenor. "AI and the Future of Geopolitics," *Brookings*, November 14, 2018, https://www.brookings.edu/blog/techtank/2018/11/14/artificial-intelligence-and-the-future-of-geopolitics/.

23   GAFAM: Google (Alphabet), Apple, Facebook, Amazon and Microsoft; NATU: Netflix, Airbnb, Tesla and Uber; BATX: Baidu, Alibaba, Tencent, and Xiaomi.

24   Drum Kevin. "Welcome to the Digital Revolution," *Foreign Affairs*, July/August 2018, https://www.foreignaffairs.com/articles/world/2018-06-14/tech-world.

25   Krishna Mrinalini. "At $ 1 Trillion, Apple Is Bigger Than These Things," *Investopedia. com*, August 2, 2018, https://www.investopedia.com/news/apple-now-bigger-these-5-things/, and The World Bank. "Gross Domestic Product, 2017," http://databank. worldbank.org/data/download/GDP.pdf.
26   Hannah Bolland. "Britain Faces and AI Brain Drain as Tech Giants Raid Top Universities," *The Telegraph*, September 2, 2018, https://www.telegraph.co.uk/technology/2018/09/02/britain-faces-artificial-intelligence-brain-drain/.
27   Statista. "Internet of Things (IoT) Connected Devices Installed Base Worldwide from 2015 to 2025 (in Billions)," *Statista*, 2018, https://www.statista.com/statistics/471264/iot-number-of-connected-devices-worldwide/.
28   Lucas Mearian. "By 2020 There Will Be 5,200 GB of Data for Every Person on Earth," *Computer World*, December 11, 2012, http://www.computerworld.com/article/2493701/data-center/by-2020--there-will-be-5-200-gb-of-data-for-every-person-on-earth.html.
29   What's a Byte. "Megabytes, Gigabytes, Terabytes … What Are They?" *Whatsabyte.com*, accessed June 30, 2019, https://whatsabyte.com.
30   Jean-Marc Rickli. "Education Key to Managing Risk of Emerging Technology," *European CEO*, March 6, 2019, https://www.europeanceo.com/industry-outlook/education-key-to-managing-the-threats-posed-by-new-technology/.
31   Philip Chertoff. "Perils of Lethal Autonomous Weapons Systems Proliferations: Preventing Non-State Acquisition," *Geneva Center for Security Policy*, Strategic Security Analysis Paper, Issue 3, May 2018.
32   Nicholas Davis and Jean-Marc Rickli. "Submission to the Australian Council of Learned Academies and the Commonwealth Science Council on the Opportunities and Challenges Presented by Deployment of Artificial Intelligence," Melbourne, ACLO, July 25, 2018.
33   Gregory C. Allen and Taniel Chan. "Artificial Intelligence and National Security," Belfer Center for Science and International Affairs, July 2018, https://www.belfercenter.org/sites/default/files/files/publication/AI%20NatSec%20-%20final.pdf.
34   Ashleigh Stewart. "China Has Unveiled Its 'First Female AI News Anchor'," *Arts & Culture*, February 21, 2019, https://www.thenational.ae/arts-culture/china-has-unveiled-its-first-female-ai-news-anchor-1.828533.
35   David Hambling. "Zero-sum Games Are Turning AIs into Powerful Creative Tools," *Wired*, January 27, 2018, https://www.wired.co.uk/article/artificial-intelligence-will-be-a-creative-tool.
36   Samantha Cole. "We Are Truly Fucked: Everyone Is Making AI-Generated Fake Porn Now," *Motherboard*, January 24, 2018, https://www.vice.com/en_us/article/bjye8a/reddit-fake-porn-app-daisy-ridley.
37   Samantha Cole. "Deep Voice Software Can Clone Anyone's Voice with Just 3.7 Seconds of Audio," *Motherboard*, March 7, 2018, https://motherboard.vice.com/en_us/article/3k7mgn/baidu-deep-voice-software-can-clone-anyones-voice-with-just-37-seconds-of-audio.
38   Patrick Tucker. "The Newest AI-Enabled Weapon: Deepfaking Photos of the Earth," *Defence One*, March 31, 2019, https://www.defenseone.com/technology/2019/03/next-phase-ai-deep-faking-whole-world-and-china-ahead/155944/.

39    Karen Hao. "You Can Train an AI to Fake UN Speeches in 13 Hours," *MIT Technology Review*, June 7, 2019, https://www.technologyreview.com/f/613645/ai-fake-news-deepfakes-misinformation-united-nations/.

40    BBC. "Computer Virus Alters Cancer Scan Images," *BBC*, April 4, 2019, https://www.bbc.com/news/technology-47812475.

41    Samantha Cole. "This Horrible App Undresses a Photo of Any Woman with a Single Click," *Motherboard*, June 16, 2019, https://www.vice.com/en_us/article/kzm59x/deepnude-app-creates-fake-nudes-of-any-woman.

42    Henry Kissinger. "How the Enlightenment Ends," *The Atlantic*, June 2018, https://www.theatlantic.com/magazine/toc/2018/06/.

43    Andreas Krieg and Jean-Marc Rickli. *Surrogate Warfare: The Transformation of War in the Twenty-First Century.* Georgetown: Georgetown University Press, 2019.

44    Defense Science Board. *Summer Study on Autonomy.* Washington, Department of Defense, Office of the Under Secretary of Defense for Acquisition, Technology and Logistics, June 2016, pp. iii and 3.

45    Miles Brundage et al. *The Malicious Use of Artificial Intelligence: Forecasting, Prevention, and Mitigation,* February 2018, p. 21, https://arxiv.org/pdf/1802.07228.

46    Miles Brundage et al. *The Malicious Use of Artificial Intelligence: Forecasting, Prevention, and Mitigation,* February 2018, p. 18, https://arxiv.org/pdf/1802.07228.

47    James M. Acton. "Reclaiming Strategic Stability," in Elbridge A. Colby and Michael S. Gerson (eds.), *Strategic Stability: Contending Interpretations.* Carlisle Barracks, PA: U.S. Army War College Press, 2013, p. 117.

48    Vincent Boulanin. "The Future of Machine Learning and Autonomy in Nuclear Weapon Systems," in Vincent Boulanin (ed.), *The Impact of Artificial Intelligence on Strategic Stability and Nuclear Risk.* Stockholm: SIPRI, Volume I (Euro-Atlantic Perspectives), 2019, p. 57, https://www.sipri.org/sites/default/files/2019-05/sipri1905-ai-strategic-stability-nuclear-risk.pdf.

49    Michael C. Horowitz "Artificial Intelligence and Nuclear Stability," in Vincent Boulanin (ed.), *The Impact of Artificial Intelligence on Strategic Stability and Nuclear Risk.* Stockholm: SIPRI, Volume I (Euro-Atlantic Perspectives), 2019, pp. 80–81, https://www.sipri.org/sites/default/files/2019-05/sipri1905-ai-strategic-stability-nuclear-risk.pdf.

50    Horowitz, Michael C. "Artificial Intelligence and Nuclear Stability," in Vincent Boulanin (ed.), *The Impact of Artificial Intelligence on Strategic Stability and Nuclear Risk.* Stockholm: SIPRI, Volume I (Euro-Atlantic Perspectives), 2019, p. 81, https://www.sipri.org/sites/default/files/2019-05/sipri1905-ai-strategic-stability-nuclear-risk.pdf.

51    Michael C. Horowitz "Artificial Intelligence and Nuclear Stability," in Vincent Boulanin (ed.), *The Impact of Artificial Intelligence on Strategic Stability and Nuclear Risk.* Stockholm: SIPRI, Volume I (Euro-Atlantic Perspectives), 2019, p. 82, https://www.sipri.org/sites/default/files/2019-05/sipri1905-ai-strategic-stability-nuclear-risk.pdf.

52    Jean-Marc Rickli. "The Destabilizing Prospects of Artificial Intelligence for Nuclear Strategy, Deterrence, and Stability," in Vincent Boulanin (ed.), *The Impact of Artificial Intelligence on Strategic Stability and Nuclear Risk.* Stockholm: SIPRI, Volume I (Euro-Atlantic Perspectives), 2019, pp. 91–98, https://www.sipri.org/sites/default/files/2019-05/sipri1905-ai-strategic-stability-nuclear-risk.pdf.

53    Edward Geist and Andrew Lohn. *How Might Artificial Intelligence Affect the Risk of Nuclear War?* Santa Monica: Rand Corporation, 2018, p. 11, https://www.rand.org/pubs/perspectives/PE296.html.

54   Zachary S. Davis. "Artificial Intelligence on the Battlefield: An Initial Survey of the Potential Implications for Deterrence, Stability and Strategic Surprise," Lawrence Livermore National Laboratory, March 2019, p. 16, https://cgsr.llnl.gov/content/assets/docs/CGSR-AI_BattlefieldWEB.pdf.

55   Pavel Sharikov. "Artificial Intelligence, Cyberattack, and Nuclear Weapons: A Dangerous Combination," *Bulletin of the Atomic Scientists*, vol. 74, issue 6, 2018, p. 371, https://www.tandfonline.com/doi/full/10.1080/00963402.2018.1533185?instNam e=University+of+Glasgow.

56   Marc Ph. Stoecklin. "DeepLocker: How AI Can Power a Stealthy New Breed of Malware," *Security Intelligence*, August 8, 2018, https://securityintelligence.com/deeplocker-how-ai-can-power-a-stealthy-new-breed-of-malware/.

57   Pavel Sharikov. "Artificial Intelligence, Cyberattack, and Nuclear Weapons: A Dangerous Combination," *Bulletin of the Atomic Scientists*, vol. 74, issue 6, 2018, pp. 370–71, https://www.tandfonline.com/doi/full/10.1080/00963402.2018.1533185?instN ame=University+of+Glasgow.

58   Pavel Sharikov. "Artificial Intelligence, Cyberattack, and Nuclear Weapons: A Dangerous Combination," *Bulletin of the Atomic Scientists*, vol. 74, issue 6, 2018, p. 370, https://www.tandfonline.com/doi/full/10.1080/00963402.2018.1533185?instNam e=University+of+Glasgow.

59   Scharre P. Paul. *Robotics on the Battlefield Part II: The Coming Swarm*, Washington: Center for a New American Security, October 2014.

60   Jürgen Altman and Frank Sauer. "Autonomous Weapons Systems and Strategic Stability," *Survival*, vol. 59, issue 5, 2017, pp. 117–42.

61   Jean-Marc Rickli. "The Impact of Autonomy and Artificial Intelligence on Strategic Stability," *UN Special*, July–August 2018, pp. 32–33, https://www.unspecial.org/2018/07/the-impact-of-autonomy-and-artificial-intelligence-on-strategic-stability/, and Jean-Marc Rickli. "The Impact of Autonomous Weapons Systems on International Security and Strategic Stability," in Quentin Ladetto (ed.), *Defence Future Technologies: What We See on the Horizon*. Thun: Armasuisse, 2017, pp. 61–64, https://deftech.ch/What-We-See-On-The-Horizon/armasuisseW%2BT_Defence-Future-Technologies-What-We-See-On-The-Horizon-2017_HD.pdf.

62   Some interpretations of customary law allow for a limited right to preemptive self-defense based on interpretation of article 51 of the UN Charter when an attack is imminent and inevitable.

63   Jean-Marc Rickli. "The Impact of Autonomy and Artificial Intelligence on Strategic Stability," *UN Special*, July–August 2018, pp. 32–33, https://www.unspecial.org/2018/07/the-impact-of-autonomy-and-artificial-intelligence-on-strategic-stability/.

64   John Borrie. "Cold War Lessons for Automation in Nuclear Weapons System," in Vincent Boulanin (ed.), *The Impact of Artificial Intelligence on Strategic Stability and Nuclear Risk*. Stockholm: SIPRI, Volume I (Euro-Atlantic Perspectives), 2019, pp. 41–52, https://www.sipri.org/sites/default/files/2019-05/sipri1905-ai-strategic-stability-nuclear-risk.pdf.

65   Jean-Marc Rickli. "The Economic, Security and Military Implications of Artificial Intelligence for the Gulf Arab States," *Emirates Diplomatic Academy Policy Paper*, Abu Dhabi, November 2018, p. 9, http://eda.ac.ae/docs/default-source/Publications/eda-insight_ai_en.pdf.

# Part II
# AI AND ECONOMIC DEVELOPMENT

# Chapter 6

# USING AI TO IMPROVE ECONOMIC PRODUCTIVITY: A BUSINESS MODEL PERSPECTIVE

Oleksiy Osiyevskyy, Yongjian Bao, and Carlos M. Dasilva

## Introduction

Since its inception in the 1950s, the progress of artificial intelligence (AI) technologies culminated in the development of a particular subfield, machine learning, to such level that nowadays it dramatically reshapes the business practices across industries. The term "machine learning" refers to algorithmic systems that automatically and progressively improve their performance on a specific task with experience (Samuel, 1959). These systems turned out to be particularly useful for generating accurate statistical predictions from available data (Agrawal et al., 2018), thus providing the essential input for managerial decision-making.

The work of managers that determines the course of society comprises essentially decision-making tasks, such as defining agendas, setting goals, designing actions, and evaluating and choosing from possible alternatives (Simon et al., 1987). All these cognitive tasks are based on processing the available information, and this is where the predictions and help of machine learning systems can substantially change the practices and resulting effectiveness and efficiency of the economic activity. Even though one might argue that in addition to making decisions the managers must also ensure their implementation, we will show that in this realm the AI technologies are also going to have a profound, transformational impact.

Today's machine learning technologies embedded in computer systems with ever-increasing power allow gaining nuanced insights from existing data, spotting hidden patterns, and generating meaningful predictions that get better as more data become available. The usefulness of machine learning

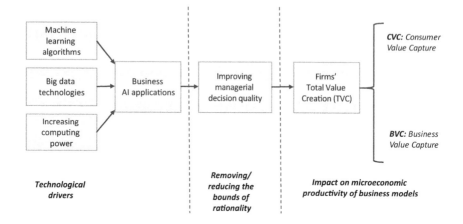

**Figure 6.1** The impact of AI technologies on firm-level productivity.

is thus augmented by the availability of data to learn from (Siegel, 2016). Consequently, these machine learning technologies become particularly useful when combined with big data technologies (i.e., collecting large volumes of unstructured data about social phenomena (McAfee et al., 2012), yielding unprecedented insights that can be used to assist managerial decision-making. As a result, AI technologies have the potential to drastically reshape business operations and to provide multiple new opportunities, thus having a profound impact on management practice with respect to firm-level microeconomic mechanisms of value creation and capture, that is, organizational business models (Biloshapka et al., 2016; Osiyevskyy and Zargarzadeh, 2015).

To date, the impact of AI on the effectiveness and efficiency of organizational business models remains poorly understood. We hope this chapter will throw light on the subject and open avenues for further research. The summary of our argument is presented in Figure 6.1.

## Business AI Applications: Drivers and Immediate Outcomes

### Technological drivers of business AI applications

The growing use and effectiveness of AI systems in business are driven by a combination of three interrelated technological trends: (1) increasing power of computer systems combined with the advancements and affordability of distributed, scalable computing and data storage enabled through cloud technology (DaSilva et al., 2013), (2) advances in machine learning algorithms, and (3) increasing accumulation and availability of multiple datasets to learn from, commonly known as "big data."

Effectuated by these technological trends, the rising effectiveness of AI applications in business will substantively improve the quality of predictions (Agrawal et al., 2018; Siegel, 2016) and corresponding quality of managerial decision-making, along with enabling the knowledge transfer (most important, the tacit one) between business systems. The improvement in the quality of decision-making and knowledge transfer capability will lead to a reduction and possible elimination of the fundamental micro-foundational management problem—bounded rationality of human decision-makers (Simon, 1955). This impact is the most immediate and direct outcome of business AI applications, followed by a domino effect that will impact the microeconomic productivity of firms' business models.

### *AI and bounded rationality problem*

One of the major contributions of Herbert Simon to contemporary management science is the concept of managerial bounded rationality (e.g., Simon, 1955). This fundamental assumption stresses the scarcity of mind of real-world decision-makers, who operate predominantly in "satisficing" mode (i.e., finding a good enough solution because of cognitive limitations), rather than trying to get to the optimal solution provided from the available information (i.e., idealistic "optimizing" mode of the conventional models of rational choice). Despite human decision-makers' best efforts, their cognitive capabilities are limited, and as such the allocated attention and time for managerial decision-making cannot be sufficient for analyzing all available information. Alas, this discrepancy between satisficing and optimizing becomes more salient with the advent of information coming from the big data technologies.

The ever-increasing power of today's computer systems removes or substantively alleviates the computational limitations that would otherwise constrain the "cognitive capacity" of AI algorithms, which can now formulate optimal or very close to optimal (rather than "good enough," satisficing) solutions within the boundaries of the available information, for most kinds of problems being solved in management. Moreover, as big data technologies yield more information for machine learning, the quality of AI's solutions tends to improve substantively, allowing to capitalize on all trends, weak signals, and predictive patterns in the data, no matter how small. Of course, after a certain threshold of data availability to learn from, when all crucial patterns were already noticed by the AI system, the marginal improvement in AI decision-making quality reduces as the magnitude of the newly uncovered patterns and effects diminish. This creates the sigmoid shape of the "machine decision-making" curve (see Figure 6.2).

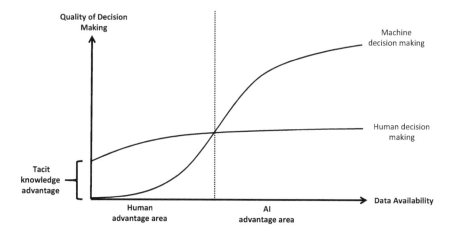

**Figure 6.2** The impact of data availability on quality of machine and human decision-making.

In contrast, the quality of human solutions remains the same or improves marginally with more data (or in some cases even worsens (Goldstein and Gigerenzer, 2008)), as the limited cognitive capacity of humans prevents them from fully utilizing additional data inputs. Human actors can notice and take into account only most salient emerging patterns, and the additional data to learn from does not affect the quality of a human decision after a certain threshold (see the "human decision-making" curve in Figure 6.2).

However, in the decision-making process, the managers rely not only on the available explicit information and knowledge relevant for the decision at hand but also on the substantive amount of "tacit" knowledge (Polanyi, 1966) gained with experience, which is hard to transfer to other managers or AI systems. This tacit knowledge ingrained in experienced managers tends to give them a major advantage over AI systems when there are few data points to learn from. However, as more data become available for AI processing, this advantage becomes less pronounced and tends to dissipate (see Figure 6.2).

As such, the availability of data to learn and make inferences from creates a natural separation line or "division of decision" in firms. Human managers' advantage (stemming from their tacit knowledge and experience) falls in the region of low data availability. AI advantage starts in the region where sufficient data are available. Indeed, a crucial limitation of AI systems today is their context specificity. Patterns learned by an algorithm in one context (say, banking industry) cannot be transferred to another (e.g., healthcare). Yet, once the context is determined and data scientists set the system to learn from the big data, the human advantage quickly gives way to the machine advantage.

## Business AI Applications: Impact on Microeconomic Productivity

### *Value-based view on the business models*

As discussed, AI systems trained on big data ultimately allow alleviating or substantively reducing the bounds of organizational decision-makers' rationality, thus leading to improvement in firms' microeconomic productivity, reflected in the value created and captured through their business models (see Figure 6.1).

A firm's business model is the system of interrelated, routinized activities within the organization, serving the purpose of creating the value for consumers and capturing the value for its shareholders (Osiyevskyy and Zargarzadeh, 2015; Biloshapka et al., 2016; Massa et al., 2017). On a broader level, a business model is a fundamental organization-level unit through which the firm as an economic entity creates value in a market society. In particular, the total value created (TVC) by a firm's business model is defined as the difference between consumers' aggregate willingness to pay (WTP) for the offering of the firm's value proposition and the aggregated costs (C) that the firm incurs for delivering on the promises of the value proposition (Brandenburger and Stuart, 1996; Biloshapka and Osiyevskyy, 2018):

$$TVC = WTP - C \tag{1}$$

The TVC construct defines the total microeconomic surplus (value) created by the firm's business model. Any factors (including AI-enabled) that can drive up the WTP or drive down C will increase the firm's value creation (surplus) in the economy. The created surplus is then distributed through the mechanism of average price (P) between the consumers (consumer value captured, CVC = WTP − P) and the firm (business value captured, BVC = P − C) (refer to Figure 6.3).

$$TVC = CVC + BVC = (WTP - P) + (P - C) = WTP - C \tag{2}$$

This disaggregation of the microeconomic value created and captured through a firm's business model allows analyzing the impact of AI technologies on microeconomic productivity. For this, we explicitly link the parameters of the business model's microeconomic value (WTP, P, C, defining the resulting

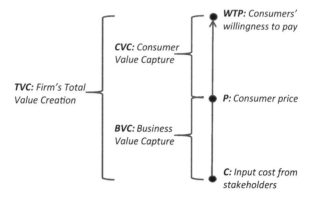

**Figure 6.3**  Value creation and capture in a firm's business model.
*Source*: Adapted from Brandenburger and Stuart (1996) and Biloshapka and Osiyevskyy (2018).

customer and business value (CVC, BVC)) with the AI-enabled improvements in quality of managerial decision-making.

### AI technologies augmenting WTP

WTP reflects the maximum monetary value (estimated amount of money, other valuable goods or services, or personal time) a potential consumer is willing to sacrifice in order to acquire the firm's product or service. WTP reflects the perceived, subjective evaluation of the benefits obtained from an exchange with the firm, constrained by the consumer's wealth. The organizational business model affects the consumers' WTP through its *value proposition* (Biloshapka and Osiyevskyy, 2018), or the set of promised benefits, for example, performance, ease of use, reliability, flexibility, and affectivity (Lindič and DaSilva, 2011). As such, the firm can increase the consumers' WTP through better adjusting its value proposition to their needs, passions, desires, and individual consequences. In the pre-AI era, traditional market segmentation was limited by the bounded rationality of sales and marketing managers. The value proposition was kept standard within each customer segment, ignoring the within-segment consumer heterogeneity. In contrast, AI technologies allow reducing the segment size to a single customer (a "microtargeting" phenomenon; Murray and Scime (2010)), ensuring that the value proposition matches his or her individually predicted requirements, thus boosting the resulting WTP. For example, a large player in the Chinese banking industry ("Alpha") was traditionally deriving its competitive advantage from a nuanced understanding of the individual customers' preferences, offering tailored banking services and pricing. In the pre-AI era, the state-of-the-art IT system generating customer's offers was based on a single analytical equation with 200 variables. As powerful as it was, the system still was able to accommodate only very limited amount of information for predicting the best offer, with large amounts of customer data (including about the individual transactions) being ignored or used as part of broad aggregates. The shift to the AI approach for generating value propositions and pricing allowed the bank to accommodate all available information that it had about its customers, reaching up to 40 million predictors in certain cases. The machine learning approach for segmentation and positioning, therefore, allowed the firm to fully utilize the available big data, leading to insights that were not possible in the pre-AI era. For example, by analyzing the frequency of advancing small amounts of cash to a particular customer, the machine intelligence was able to detect the male customer's wife's pregnancy and relate it to an application for an auto loan. A post hoc sensemaking explanation is that anticipating a baby encourages young fathers to think about purchasing a new car. Predictions like this empower the bank to offer a new series of financial products with differentiated pricing—all suited to a customer's particular life circumstances.

Moreover, since WTP is a subjective assessment of the firm's value proposition, AI technologies can be successfully used to increase this subjective evaluation in the consumers' minds through predicting the most effective way to convey customer-focused value propositions, for example, in automatically managed ads and promotion activities.

Finally, in addition to making sure that the value proposition is adjusted to individual consumers and properly communicated, there is a fundamental need of selecting the consumers that would appreciate the firm's offering most, that is, *value targeting* (Biloshapka and Osiyevskyy, 2018). Here, the power of AI-enabled decision-making substantively surpasses the best practice yet boundedly rational approach of human marketing managers, who despite best efforts cannot analyze massive amounts of big data for weak signals. For example, the experimental results for mobile Internet users' renewal rates (Sundsøy et al., 2014) demonstrated that the AI-powered approach generated 13 times better conversion rate compared to the control group (traditional best practice marketing). Furthermore, the AI-selected group demonstrated a 98 percent renewal rate, as compared to 37 percent in the control group.

### AI technologies reducing costs

The variable C in equation 1 reflects the firm's total costs incurred when operating its business model. For the purposes of our analysis, the total costs can be disaggregated into: (1) costs of customer acquisition and (2) costs of serving the customers.

The AI models can successfully improve managerial decision-making with respect to reducing the costs of customer acquisition. The predictive models ensure that the firm's marketing, promotion, and customer retention efforts are reaching their maximum potential. For example, Siegel (2016) reports how AI-powered systems allowed Life Line Screening to increase its direct mail marketing campaign response rate by 38 percent while cutting costs by 28 percent. Similarly, the payroll processing firm Paychex employed AI predictive model that resulted in a 40 percent decrease in the average number of phone calls necessary to book a sales meeting, hence dramatically increasing the direct sales efficiency.

Furthermore, AI systems have proven to increase the efficiency of the firms' operations (procurement, logistics, manufacturing, service), thus reducing the costs of serving the customers. Examples of the power of AI systems here are numerous (Siegel, 2016), such as UPS cutting 85 million driven miles annually by employing a semiautomatic, prediction-based scheduling and routing system. Similarly, Hewlett-Packard is reported to benefit from an estimated $300 million in potential savings due to their prediction system that signals "flight risk," meaning high chances of an employee quitting his or her job. The McKinsey & Company (2017) report documents AI-enabled cost savings across a range of industries, such as 20 percent stock reduction in retail, 39 percent IT staff reduction due to fully automated procurement processes, and 30–50 percent productivity increase of nurses supported by AI tools.

### AI technologies setting the price right

Finally, the TVC by a business model is distributed between consumers and the firm through the mechanism of average price (P) (Figure 6.3). The proper AI-powered pricing strategy, by adjusting the price to the predicted characteristics of each individual customer, could allow a firm to maximize its value capture. For example, in the case of the "Alpha" bank, the AI-based prediction of the preferences and available wealth of a particular customer allows determining fairly accurately the WTP for a certain offer, thus enabling proper pricing.

### Conclusion

In summary, AI technologies are rapidly entering all spheres of business and are here to stay. The primary goal of this study is in demonstrating a set of mechanisms through which AI technologies will affect management practices across industries. We predict that AI technologies are likely to drastically reshape the organization of commercial enterprises in the short to medium term.

On a more fundamental level, as soon as sufficient "big data" becomes available across industries, our business practices will move to the era of "AI advantage" (Figure 6.2), where most business decisions—both operational and strategic—will be better made by AI systems than by human experts. Questions of proper market positioning, selecting the right technologies, choosing the right market entry strategies, and many others will be reliant on AI systems. This requires rethinking of business schools' curricula, as well as preparing the current generation of managers for a new era. However, we are far from forecasting a "gloomy" future for human managers. If we are willing incorporate AI systems in our firms in order to make them more efficient, managers and AI systems will become partners reinforcing each other's strengths (Davenport and Kirby, 2016), complementing rather than substituting each other.

## References

Agrawal, A., Gans, J., and Goldfarb, A. (2018). *Prediction Machines: The Simple Economics of Artificial Intelligence*. Boston, MA: Harvard Business Review Press.

Biloshapka, V., and Osiyevskyy, O. (2018). Value creation mechanisms of business models: proposition, targeting, appropriation, and delivery. *International Journal of Entrepreneurship and Innovation*, 19(3), 166–76.

Biloshapka, V., Osiyevskyy, O., and Meyer, M. H. (2016). The value matrix: a tool for assessing the future of a business model. *Strategy & Leadership*, 44(4), 41–48.

Brandenburger, A. M., and Stuart, H. W. (1996). Value-based business strategy. *Journal of Economics & Management Strategy*, 5(1), 5–24.

DaSilva, C. M., Trkman, P., Desouza, K., and Lindič, J. (2013). Disruptive technologies: a business model perspective on cloud computing. *Technology Analysis & Strategic Management*, 25(10), 1161–173.

Davenport, T. H., and Kirby, J. (2016). *Only Humans need Apply: Winners and Losers in the Age of Smart Machines*. New York: Harper Business.

Goldstein, D. G., and Gigerenzer, G. (2008). The recognition heuristic and the less-is-more effect. *Handbook of Experimental Economics Results*, 1, 987–92.

Lindič, J., and DaSilva, C. (2011). Value proposition as a catalyst for a customer focused innovation. *Management Decision*, 49(10), 1694–708.

Massa, L., Tucci, C. L., and Afuah, A. (2017). A critical assessment of business model research. *Academy of Management Annals*, 11(1), 73–104.

McAfee, A., Brynjolfsson, E., Davenport, T. H., Patil, D. J., and Barton, D. (2012). Big data: the management revolution. *Harvard Business Review*, 90(10), 60–68.

McKinsey & Company (2017). *Artificial Intelligence: The Next Digital Frontier?* McKinsey Global Institute Discussion Paper.

Murray, G. R., and Scime, A. (2010). Microtargeting and electorate segmentation: data mining the American National Election Studies. *Journal of Political Marketing*, 9(3), 143–66.

Osiyevskyy, O., and Zargarzadeh, M. A. (2015). Business model design and innovation in the process of expansion and growth of global enterprises, in A. A. Camillo (Ed.), *Global Enterprise Management: New Perspectives on Challenges and Future Development* (v. 1). New York: Palgrave Macmillan, pp. 115–33.

Polanyi, M. (1966). *The Tacit Dimension*. London: Routledge.

Samuel, A. L. (1959). Some studies in machine learning using the game of checkers. *IBM Journal of Research and Development*, 3(3), 210–29.

Siegel, E. (2016). *Predictive Analytics: The Power to Predict Who will Click, Buy, Lie, or Die* (Revised and Updated Edition). Hoboken, New Jersey: John Wiley.

Simon, H. (1955). A behavioral model of rational choice. *Quarterly Journal of Economics*, 69(1), 99–118.

Simon, H. A., Dantzig, G. B., Hogarth, R., Plott, C. R., Raiffa, H., Schelling, T. C., Shepsle, K. A., Thaler, R., Tversky, A., and Winter, S. (1987). Decision making and problem solving. *Interfaces*, 17(5), 11–31.

Sundsøy, P., Bjelland, J., Iqbal, A. M., and de Montjoye, Y. A. (2014). Big data-driven marketing: how machine learning outperforms marketers' gut-feeling, in A. M. Greenberg, W. G. Kennedy, and N. D. Bos (Eds.) *International Conference on Social Computing, Behavioral-Cultural Modeling, and Prediction*. Cham: Springer, pp. 367–74.

# Chapter 7

# HANDLING RESULTANT UNEMPLOYMENT FROM ARTIFICIAL INTELLIGENCE

## Margaret A. Goralski and Krystyna Górniak-Kocikowska

This chapter on handling resultant unemployment from artificial intelligence (AI) begins with the Obama report of October 2016, delves into the concerns of the G7 (Canada, France, Germany, Italy, Japan, the United Kingdom, and the United States) ministerial meeting on preparing for jobs of the future, explores the developments in AI and governmental policy in the Trump administration, and incorporates the findings of the World Economic Forum, Future of Jobs, Global Competitiveness, and Global Gender Gap Reports 2018.

When former US president Barack Obama chartered the National Science and Technology Council (NSTC) subcommittee on Machine Learning and Artificial Intelligence in May 2016, it was specifically created to provide technical and policy advice on topics related to AI and "to monitor the development of AI technologies across industry, research community, and the Federal Government" (Holdren and Smith, 2016). Information gathered by the White House Office of Science and Technology Policy (OSTP) at five public workshops was also included in this same document entitled *Preparing for the Future of Artificial Intelligence*. A subcommittee on Networking and Information Technology Research and Development (NITRD) was charged with creating a companion document *National Artificial Intelligence Research and Development Strategic Plan* to establish a set of objectives for federally funded AI research and development.

President Obama realized that as advances in technology opened up new markets and opportunities for some, there would also be an inherent risk that machine learning and AI would surpass human performance in specific skills and potentially could become comparable to, or exceed, human performance in skills and intelligence. This is a matter of serious concern, expressed by many in recent years. Most notably, it was brought to the public in August 2015 when Stephen Hawking, Steve Wozniak, Elon Musk, Bill Gates, and hundreds of others voiced their concern about a future super-intelligence of AI in relationship to the slow biological process of humans (Ashafian, 2015; Bostrom, 2008; Goralski and Górniak-Kocikowska, 2014, 2017, 2018; Goralski and O'Connor, 2018; Sainato, 2015).

Of course, AI is here to stay and it could contribute to economic growth and be a valuable tool for governments around the world as long as the risks and challenges that AI represents are recognized by government, industry, and society. It will be important to ensure that everyone has an opportunity to help create this new AI-enhanced society and benefit from these new scientific and technological developments. This will be the ultimate challenge.

The abovementioned Obama report discusses the use of AI in the critical areas of healthcare, education, energy, and the environment as some of the new markets and opportunities that have been created for progress and for the betterment of life conditions of millions of humans. "One area of great optimism about AI and machine learning is their potential to improve people's lives by helping to solve some of the world's greatest challenges and inefficiencies" (Holdren and Smith, 2016: v). However, one must also recognize that for each of the problems that is solved by machine learning or AI, a human has given up his/her ability to solve that specific problem. Hence it is easy to see how, with time, AI could become more intelligent and humans less intelligent. When we, as humans, decide to allow machine learning or AI to solve some of the world's greatest challenges and inefficiencies, then we concede to give up that right. When we allow IBM's Watson to make a determination about a specific health treatment for a family member, then we have reduced the intelligence of human doctors down to implementors of solutions rather than solvers of problems. We have diminished the intellectual capability of humans. It is, therefore, crucial not to think in terms of "humans or machines," but rather of humans and machines working together, possibly in partnership.

While government has a role to play in advancing AI, it also has a role to play in maximizing and building a highly trained workforce of people who have the skills necessary to support and advance the field of AI. While in the short term AI is automating tasks previously performed by humans, in the long term, as AI will make decisions about people and possibly replace decisions made currently by human-driven processes, there are concerns about government's ability to ensure a just, fair, and accountable system. The outlook for people in lower-wage jobs will be at high risk for replacement. The wage gap between less-educated and more-educated workers could, and probably will, increase economic inequality across large segments of the world population. Unintended consequences of widespread adoption of AI technologies have been raised by many ethicists, policy analysts, as well as technical experts. As use of AI is considered for implementation in ever-expanding areas of industry, education and governmental safety nets need to keep pace in understanding and adapting to a rapidly changing world.

The G7 Ministers of Employment and Innovation met in Montréal in March 2018 to discuss globalization and emerging technologies and to understand how the changing economy would impact industries and workers. In addition, the discussion focused on how each of their governments could help citizens adapt and thrive as fundamental shifts take place in their economies and labor markets. The resulting report highlights more specific segments of the population that will be affected by implementation of machine learning and AI. These include increased gender inequality with specific recommendations for women to study and seek careers in the fields of science, technology, engineering, and mathematics (STEM). This may be the ideal; however, it will not quickly be the reality. The ministers highlighted the importance of incorporating gender analysis into government budgeting and programming to set metrics and track results to meet governmental objectives of equality and to increase the empowerment of women. "Societies cannot afford to lose out on the skills, ideas and perspectives of half of humanity to realize the promise of a more prosperous and human-centric future that well-governed innovation and technology can bring" (Schwab, 2018b: para. 2).

Ministers are determined to invest in digital literacy as well as foundational and social skills by collaborating with the private sector, education, and industry. The G7 ministers are considering measures such as apprenticeships and training opportunities as well as adult upskilling programs. These measures in addition to pay equity to reach specified goals are in line with the UN 2030 Agenda for Sustainable Development—people, planet, prosperity, peace, and partnership (United Nations Transforming Our World: The 2030 Agenda for Sustainable Development, n.d.).

An increased need for STEM knowledge and education was also recommended in the Obama report of 2016, albeit not specifically for women. The Obama report recommends STEM implementation in elementary education from kindergarten through twelfth grade (K–12). However, not all people of the world will be capable of pursuing a STEM education and fulfilling this prophecy for inclusion in future economic prosperity. The G7 suggestion of apprenticeships, training opportunities, and adult upskilling programs is more specifically on the mark for inclusion of people from all segments of the population to benefit from growth generated from innovation. Klaus Schwab, founder and executive chairman of the World Economic Forum, states:

> The inherent opportunities for economic prosperity, societal progress and individual flourishing in this new world of work are enormous yet depend crucially on the ability of all concerned stakeholders to instigate reform in education and training systems, labour market policies, business approaches to developing skills, employment arrangements and existing social contracts. (2018a: v)

The G7 Innovation Ministers articulated a vision of human-centric AI for key areas like economics, governance, health, and security. The US government, the G7 Ministers, and the World Economic Forum are all in agreement that efforts must be made to invest in collaborative innovation systems, improve access to capital, adopt technology, invest in R&D, enable firms to tap into global talent pools, and streamline governmental programs. Stakeholders in these future developments include academics, governments, policymakers, private sector partners, and specialists in the field of innovation. However, equally or perhaps even more important to the future development and deployment of AI are economic, ethical, legal, and social issues that will break down the barriers and allow the labor force to participate, collaborate, and support these innovations and investments.

The stakeholders involved in these crucial decisions unfortunately do not function harmoniously on the same timeline. Industry sets the pace and others follow, hence the great importance of the World Economic Forum, which gathers collective knowledge on trends in employment skills and human capital investments across industries and countries (Schwab, 2018a). While whole new job categories are expected to be created in the future based on technological innovation, there will also be a reduction of workers for specific tasks that are performed better and faster by big data analytics, robotics, and/or AI. For millions of workers worldwide, difficult transitions will require development of lifelong learners and skilled talent. Since industry moves at a more rapid pace than government, it will be important for industry to take an active role in supporting its existing workforce through reskilling and upskilling. It is also important that employees take a proactive stance on their own lifelong learning and ability to move into these technologically innovative positions as they become available. While governments can assist in these efforts, the challenge to create a workforce strategy for the future will depend on industry recognizing that capital investment in human resources will allow new technology adoption, job creation, and leveraging of their own motivated and agile workforce (Schwab, 2018).

In March 2019, US President Trump and Vice President Pence attended the inaugural meeting of the American Workforce Policy Advisory Board. The Board's objective is to "leverage the knowledge of its members to develop and implement a strategy to revamp the American workforce to better meet the challenges of the 21st century" (Office of the Governor of Iowa, 2019: para. 1). The Board, which is cochaired by Secretary of Commerce Wilbur Ross and Advisor to the President Ivanka Trump, includes diverse members from the private sector, educational institutions, and local and state governments. The four goals that are the mandate of the council include:

> To develop a robust campaign to promote multiple pathways to good-paying jobs, dispelling the myth that there is only one path to a successful career. Second, improving the availability of high-quality, transparent, and timely data to better inform students and educators, as well as match American workers to American jobs. Third, modernizing candidate recruitment and training practices to expand the pool of job applicants [that] employers are looking to hire. And finally, measuring and encouraging employer-led training and investments. We are championing and seeking to further private-sector leadership and investment in workforce development. (Remarks by President Trump at an American Workforce Policy Advisory Board Meeting, 2019: paras 4–7)

The board also seeks to influence the legislative agenda to summon higher education to be more responsive to today's students and entrepreneurial creators of new jobs. Apple CEO Tim Cook, a member of the American Workforce Policy Advisory Board, stated that there is a mismatch between the skills that students who are graduating from college possess and the skills that he believes are needed for the future. One of those skills has been identified as coding. Cook believes that coding should be a requirement in the United States for every child from kindergarten to grade 12. He believes that it is a competency for which students should become proficient. Apple has initiated this program into four thousand schools in the United States and 80 community colleges. Kim Reynolds, governor of Iowa, another member of the advisory board, stated that Iowa has initiated registered apprenticeship programs and will launch six computer science classes to target high-poverty, high-needs students. And board member Sean McGarvey, president of the North America Building and Trades Union, stated that it had made a commitment to train 250,000 new apprentices over a five-year period with 56,000 being registered with the Department of Labor in 2018. For additional information on the American Workforce Policy Advisory Board Meeting, please refer to the article titled "Remarks by President Trump at an American

Workforce Policy Advisory Board Meeting" (2019). Each of the members of this Advisory Board has obviously made a commitment for the advancement of the US workforce.

The mandate of the American Workforce Policy Advisory board closely follows the recommendation set forth by Klaus Schwab of the World Economic Forum, which we have outlined previously in this chapter. However, President Trump, Vice President Pence, Secretary of Commerce Wilbur Ross, and Advisor to the President Ivanka Trump are incentivizing educators, employers, union leaders, governmental agencies, and the private sector to take the lead in championing investment in workforce development by placing members of standing on this board and seeking their input, ideas, knowledge, and support.

Perhaps in support of Cook's opinion, the leaders of the College Board that administers the Scholastic Aptitude Test (SAT) college entrance exam asked themselves what skills and knowledge young people should be tested for in correlation to future success in college and in life. Their response was to master "two codes"—computer science and the US Constitution. David Coleman, president of the College Board, and Stefanie Sanford, its chief of global policy, stated:

> With computing, the internet, big data and artificial intelligence now the essential building blocks of almost every industry, any young person who can master the principles and basic coding techniques that drive computers and other devices 'will be more prepared for nearly every job' […] at the same time, the constitution forms the foundational code that gives shape to America and defines our essential liberties—it is the indispensable guide to our lives as productive citizens. (Friedman, 2019: para. 4)

As productive citizens, it is also our responsibility to continuously educate ourselves on the trends, advancements, and integration of machine learning and AI into our lives. We must be cognizant of the choices that we are making when we allow machine learning or AI to solve a problem that in the past would have been solved through the critical thinking of humans. The mandates of multiple governments, political leaders, policymakers, academics, industry, and the private sector have all stated loudly and clearly that the next generation of students and employees must keep pace with the fast movement of AI. In 2018, President Trump stated:

> We're on the verge of new technological revolutions that could improve virtually every aspect of our lives, create vast new wealth for American workers and families, and open up bold, new frontiers in science, medicine, and communication. (Artificial Intelligence for the American People, 2018: para. 1)

This is a bold statement. Most world leaders would agree with Trump's statement, perhaps not just for American workers and their families but also for citizens of their own country. They would agree with improvements of virtually every aspect of their population's lives and creation of vast wealth. However, this statement portrays only the advantages of this new technological revolution. There will also be great risks and swaths of people worldwide who will not be involved in STEM studies and research, who will not have received the education and skills needed to transcend these new frontiers, and who will be seriously questioning their and their family's future welfare.

As always, there will be winners and losers in this new technological revolution. For leaders of the Western world and more advanced countries, this new technological revolution is yet another competition. According to the Global Competitiveness Index 4.0 2018 rankings, the United States is number one in the rankings with Singapore and Germany following closely behind (Schwab, 2018c: xi). Countries worldwide are investing in this vast future of AI research, computing infrastructure, machine learning, and autonomous systems. Some governments are also investing in new knowledge, training, reskilling, and upskilling of their citizens, but other country leaders are asking industry to train, reskill, and upskill their employees. This then is subjective and could increase the gender gap.

Ultimately, handling resultant unemployment from AI will be a collective effort. There is not one worldwide safety net that will catch those who will fall through the cracks. There are immense benefits that will be realized by economies and societies that prevail in the rapid advancement of AI technologies. There will be improved efficiencies, reduced costs, and faster and better decision-making in extremely complex environments. AI can analyze and accelerate the discovery of useful patterns that will be utilized in manufacturing, security, healthcare, and other industries. Productivity could be improved and transformed in a range of sectors. Governments and policymakers are enthusiastic about the future of this new technological revolution. Countries at the forefront will gain significantly. The G7 notes that understanding AI technologies will create broad effects on society and economies, hence as the world advances these technologies it must be with a human-centric approach that is in keeping with laws, policies, and values. This will be a difficult prophecy to fulfill since AI, law, politics, and social values each advance at different timelines.

Ultimately, we believe that although well-meaning, governments and policymakers will find machine learning and AI to be too beneficial to the economy to slow its progress. Alas, slowing would put any country at a disadvantage. Therefore, to avert the resultant unemployment from AI, each man and woman must remain flexible, follow the trends of industry, invest in his/her own education, and seek training, reskilling, and upskilling opportunities from their employer.

## References

Artificial Intelligence for the American People (2018, May 10). Infrastructure and Technology Fact Sheets. Retrieved from https://www.whitehouse.gov/briefings-statements/artificial-intelligence-american-people/.

Ashrafian, H. (2015, March 26). Intelligent Robots Must Uphold Human Rights. *Nature*, 519, p. 391.

Bostrom, N. (2008). How Long Before Superintelligence? Retrieved from http://nickbostrom.com/superintelligence.html.

Creighton, J. (2018, December 12). How to Create AI That Can Safely Navigate Our World—An Interview with Andre Platzer. Retrieved from https://futureoflife.org/2018/12/12/how-to-create-ai-that-can-safely-navigate-our-world-andre-platzer/.

Friedman, T. L. (2019, February 12). "The Two Codes Your Kids Need to Know." *New York Times*. Retrieved from https://www.nytimes.com/2019/02/12/opinion/college-board-sat-ap.html.

Goralski, M. A., and Górniak-Kocikowska, K. (2014). A New Frontier in Ethics Education: Robotics. A paper presented at the Academy of International Business—Northeast Chapter Special Conference, Tianjin, China.

———. (2017). *Globalization, Codification, Automation, and Artificial Intelligence: Job Affectation.* Presented at the Academy of International Business–US–NE conference, Philadelphia, PA, October 20–21.

———. (2018, April). Permissionless Evolution of Ethics—Artificial Intelligence. In J. Mark Munoz and Al Naqvi, Eds., *Business Strategy in an Artificial Intelligence Economy*, pp. 69–78. New York: Business Expert Press.

Goralski, M. A., and O'Connor, M. (2018). *Artificial Intelligence, Open Cog, and Blockchain.* A paper presented at the Academy of International Business—US–Northeast Chapter Annual Conference, Philadelphia, PA, October 19–20.

Holdren, J. P., and Smith, M. (2016, October 12). Letter to colleagues of the Executive Office of the President, National Science and Technology Council, Assistant to the President for Science and Technology Director, Office of Science and Technology Policy and U.S. Chief Technology Officer.

Office of the Governor of Iowa. (2019). Gov. Reynolds appointed to American Workforce Policy Advisory Board. Retrieved from https://governor.iowa.gov/2019/02/gov-reynolds-appointed-to-american-workforce-policy-advisory-board.

Remarks by President Trump at an American Workforce Policy Advisory Board Meeting. (2019, March 6). Retrieved from https://www.whitehouse.gov/briefings-statements/remarks-president-trump-american-workforce-policy-advisory-board-meeting/.

Sainato, M. (2015, August 19). Stephen Hawking, Elon Musk, and Bill Gates Warn About Artificial Intelligence. Retrieved from https://observer.com/2015/08/stephen-hawking-elon-musk-and-bill-gates-warn-about-artificial-intelligence/.

Schwab, K. (2018a). Future of Jobs Report 2018 [The]. Centre for the New Economy and Society Insight Report. *World Economic Forum*. Retrieved from https://www.google.com/search?q=the+future+of+jobs+report+2018+pdf&oq=The+Future+of+Jobs+Report&aqs=chrome.3.0j69i57j0l4.9400j0j7&sourceid=chrome&ie=UTF-8.

———. (2018b). Global Gender Gap Report [The] 2018. *World Economic Forum*. Retrieved from https://www.weforum.org/reports/the-global-gender-gap-report-2018.

———. (2018c). Global Competitiveness Report [The] 2018. *World Economic Forum*. Retrieved from http://www3.weforum.org/docs/GCR2018/05FullReport/TheGlobalCompetitivenessReport2018.pdf.

United Nations Transforming Our World: The 2030 Agenda for Sustainable Development (n.d.). Retrieved from https://sustainabledevelopment.un.org/content/documents/21252030%20Agenda%20for%20Sustainable%20Development%20web.pdf.

# Chapter 8

# BUILDING TECH ZONES TO ENHANCE AI

## Melodena Stephens

Building artificial intelligence (AI)-tech zones is a complicated matter. An organically grown tech industry would follow a bottom-up approach, but a planned tech zone, a cluster, follows a top-down approach. This chapter will highlight the process of a top-down decision plan to create a productive AI-tech cluster. At the highest level, the fundamental value question to be answered is, "Why create an AI-tech zone?" Based on the analysis of several high-tech clusters and a detailed review of existing empirical research, it is possible to conclude that there are four levels of decisions to be considered for the creation of an AI-tech zone. They are (1) policy-level decisions for agenda setting; (2) management-level decisions that focus on cluster success factors; (3) the impact and control-level decisions, which provide a bounded reliability framework of operation; and (4) the feedback-level decisions that facilitate agile learning. Under policy-level decisions, there are three agenda items for consideration: the relevance of an AI-tech zone (for what purpose?); the scale question (for national consumption, export, or competitiveness); and the sandbox criteria (the safeguards and regulations you plan to put into place to enhance and protect AI usage for good). Under management-level decisions, there are four types of success factors to be considered: the anchor tenants (what type of organizations will create a fertile AI base?); the culture (how will you encourage entrepreneurship?); resources to be invested (what can you leverage and what can you build?); and the knowledge capital plan. The impact and control-level decisions center around the audit and govern-ance processes, to ensure that the objectives of an AI cluster are met. The feedback-level decisions allow for agile learnings, which can be used to inform the first three stages.

## The AI Cluster

Clusters are geographic concentrations of interconnected firms, suppliers, service providers, government and related institutions, and other associated organizations (e.g., universities, trade groups, etc.) (Porter, 1998). They exist as an array of linked industry or fields of specializations that can feed into each other, both horizontally (across organizations) and vertically (up and down the value stream). They usually are thought to be location based (though they can cross borders). Convention theories look at clusters as sources of competitive advantage for nations. Clusters evolve through many stages, mostly organically, but they can be seeded (Feldman and Francis, 2004).

However a cluster is formed, for the survival of a cluster and the firms inside, it must develop the quality of dynamism. This quality is defined as the inherent ability to improve, innovate, and upgrade itself relative to competition (Malmberg et al., 1996). The most important reasons for clusters to succeed are its ability to modify its composition and to be able to balance the ratio of science and capital over time (Häussler and Zademach, 2007). Clusters need to have some elements of open innovation (Chesbrough, 2006), which is an ability to learn and allow free flow of knowledge into and out of the firms for assimilation and creation of new knowledge that can be applied to create value.

AI is being used as an all-encompassing buzzword, but it refers to many types of high-technology advancements. AI refers to machines that can do one or more of the following, across multiple domains (Herzing, 2014; India, 2018; Pennachin and Goertzel, 2007):

(a) to sense (acquire knowledge);
(b) comprehend (apply knowledge and "think");
(c) act (reason and take decisions) at human or other higher levels of intelligence (including animal intelligence).

Though many distinctions are made, AI-tech involves cognitively inspired artificial models and man-made systems, complex machine and wired systems, and computational methodologies and software system (Agarwal et al., 2019; Wang, 2009), or simply put AI = hardware + software + data. AI is of different types (weak, narrow, or strong), depending on its scope (tasks, domain, and intelligence). AI is applicable in multiple fields—robotics, health, big data, smart cities, and so on.

At the highest level of AI or artificial general intelligence (AGI), machines have human-level intelligence or more—machines are self-aware, learn by themselves, deal with uncertainty, and take decisions without human

**Table 8.1** Differences between narrow AI and AGI

| System Characteristics | Narrow AI | AGI |
| --- | --- | --- |
| Specific data sets | Yes | No |
| Ability to adapt flexibly over time | No | Yes |
| Ability to integrate dramatically diverse data sources | No | Yes |
| Ability to deal with unforeseen situations | Sometimes | Yes |
| Ability to dialogue with humans | Minimal | Yes |
| Ability to perceive subtle data patterns | Sometimes | Yes |
| Simple algorithms | Sometimes | No |
| Small demand on computing resources | Sometimes | No |
| Requires massive human knowledge encoding effort | Sometimes | No |
| Self-learning (correcting) | Sometimes | Yes |

*Source*: Adapted from Goertzel and Pennachin (1998).

intervention (Goertzel and Pennachin, 2007; Franklin and Grasser, 1996; Maturana, 1975)—but we are not yet at this point. Weak AI is like a chatbot, it may talk intelligently but it does not have human consciousness; at the other extreme is the strong AI, which can take autonomous decisions and think like a human. Narrow AI is often very specific and excels at one task—a robot that can sort tomatoes, play chess, and so on. Voice assistants like Siri and autonomous cars also fall into the category of narrow AI as they have to be "taught" through data sets. An autonomous car needs to recognize, for example, traffic lights, other cars, pedestrians, and so on.

These definitions of different types of AI are fuzzy, but Table 8.1 may help demystify AI. Whatever the type of AI, the pace at which AI is growing is immense, and the question remains whether policy decisions are keeping up. Machine learning has been shown to have higher potential contribution to the development of AI (Cockburn et al., 2018). AI is yet to reach the human level of intelligence, though we see remarkable leaps in technology.

Because of the rapid and disruptive growth of AI technologies while developing an AI-tech cluster, there is a need to look at four critical levels of decision-making for its development (see Figure 8.1). The first is the policy level.

## Policy-Level Decisions: Agenda Setting

Clusters offer a constructive way to change the nature of the dialogue between the public and private sectors. The primary purpose of this level of decision-making is to ascertain why an AI-tech cluster would be significant for the

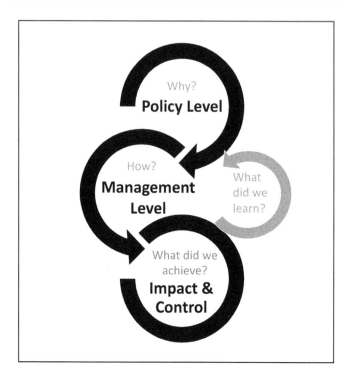

**Figure 8.1** The four-level decision-making process for AI-tech cluster development. *Source*: Author.

location. AI has enormous implications for the public as (1) AI is often built on open source platforms; (2) AI uses data from the public (with or without their permission); and (3) AI is often used for the public good (and there may be multiple perceptions on what is good). Perceptions of good raise legitimate concerns that policymakers must take into consideration from the start. Below, I highlight three policy agenda questions to be considered.

### *The relevance question—for what purpose?*

While there is a tendency to use AI to manage systems more effectively and efficiently, the question we need to ask is a simple one. *What is the purpose of the AI in the AI-tech cluster?* There are several steps in this process, which will impact the choice of AI you might want to develop, especially if you want the cluster to survive and grow.

Take, for example, the development of AI for smart cities. Smart city technology control systems will eventually act like central brains, responding to multiple levels of data. Here again, the support systems to make an AI-tech cluster competitive may be the access to a large variety and good quality of data, specialized equipment (hardware), the storage of data, and the security of the data. China currently is testing the smart city concept in more than 540 cities, which is at an unprecedented scale; most countries cannot afford it (Stephens et al., 2019). To get into this segment you need to have a realistic assessment of your country and other international players.

Using a task–technology fit approach, which is useful for decision-making (Strohmeier and Piazza, 2015), here are some questions:

1. Map the expected level of benefit for the country, which could be for internal consumption and/or exports. Evaluate which types of sectors are more open to AI adoption.
2. Evaluate if the AI builds on existing resources and competencies. In case you already have an existing cluster, you could use an AI-tech cluster to complement it. For example, the pharmaceutical cluster in the Basel region between Germany and Switzerland has 40 percent of the largest pharmaceutical companies in the world and may be an ideal ground for AI technologies in the pharmaceutical industry. If you do not have existing clusters you can leverage from, ascertain if there is true desire to attract or develop new competencies.
3. Evaluate if the proposed cluster has access to relevant data, or ownership of the data at a national level, especially if the system needs training and you wish to minimize data biases.
4. Decide what is the optimum level of infrastructure, talent, and future talent (considering cybersecurity, innovation, and tech disruptions) you will need and hence determine the gap. This needs to be cross-referenced with how much the country/location is willing to spend (time, effort, money) to develop the AI cluster.
5. Address complementariness in the development of AI-tech clusters (Porter, 1983). Complementaries are industries in the vertical and horizontal supply chain that can thrive off each other, creating a healthy ecosystem (Porter, 1998: 78). Do you wish to focus on vertical integration or horizontal integration of industries? In this case, there is a need to think of which industries will benefit from innovations of AI-tech clusters and to think of spillovers.
6. Questions should be addressing issues like the type of specialized industries you want to attract, the resources they need (access to components or raw material, talent), and whether you have a strong link to the value chain (both up and down).

The domain of AI needs to be finalized only after a critical evaluation of the resources you can use to leverage the cluster could create a competitive advantage. In this case, the AI-tech clusters should look at where data can be collected, how it will be validated, and the good governance procedures and the policy innovations required to regulate runaway innovations (think fake news). By understanding the purpose of the AI-tech cluster and the types of AI you would want to facilitate, it would be possible to create appropriate policies.

### The scale question: Where will you export?

At this stage, developments in AI are centered around the engineering or architecture problem (Goertzel and Pennachin, 2007; Franklin, 2007). The nature of the AI industry, which is instantly global (Katz et al., 2003), makes it a highly competitive sector, and there is a race to be the first in and scale internationally. From 2017 to 2018, 26 governments announced AI strategies (Dutton, 2018). AI adoption has been highest in the United States (25 percent) versus Singapore (10 percent), with all sectors having an average of 16 percent adoption rate (Küpper et al., 2018). Opportunities lie in componentry—unifying data, training AI, giving AI human features, like voice, vision, and so on, and interoperability—basically, allowing you to put AI in anything (Thomson, 2019).

The dominant design standard is still in debate. Countries with large populations may have an advantage—China, India, and Nigeria. The recent Huawei–US battle, which may be about 5G and competitiveness, makes these decisions important ones. India's National Strategy for Artificial Intelligence highlights the willingness for India to be an AI garage (India, 2018: 19): "In addition to providing unique opportunities, India provides a perfect 'playground' for enterprises and institutions globally to develop scalable solutions which can be easily implemented in the rest of the developing and emerging economies. Simply put, 'Solve for India' means solve for 40% or more of the world." AI is now embedded across many sectors (intelligence, health, marketing, retail, finance, agriculture, etc.), which makes it challenging to manage regulations across all sectors—especially if we continue to think in silos.

### The sandbox question: How will you fail safely?

AI brings with it many legal and ethical challenges. While it will no doubt lead to industry disruption at a global scale, the more significant issue is whether we are prepared for AI in terms of education of decision-makers and the consumer savvy required to understand its failability. The Facebook Cambridge

Analytica scandal showed that we are not ready yet. Experimentation and failure will be part of an AI strategy, according to Rob Thomas, IBM GM for Data and AI (Thomas, 2019; Ng, 2019).

AI is now self-learning with programs like deep learning. Often the quantity of data deep learning consumes is large, meaning that the ability to regulate it may be beyond our previously used methods. Many of the tests run for AI decision systems involve proprietary technology, which means the lessons learned are not shared. How would you create policies to overcome this?

The smart city initiatives that connect previously discrete bits of technology with each other may make us more vulnerable to security threats. Data being collected is often sourced through multiple points—being aggregated through the smart mobiles, cameras, sensors, and other touchpoints. The data, in many cases, is owned by the private sector or organizations based in another country. These raise many challenges on the ethics of getting good data, the need to make sure the data is used wisely, and the role of humans in the process. Andrew Ng cautions on AI projects and recommends that focus is on task replacement rather than job replacement (Ng, 2019). While the pace of adoption in this area is fast, the potential for misuse must be monitored and planned for.

Can we prevent AI from being misused? AI should be able to behave appropriately under unpredictable conditions, even with insufficient knowledge or resources (Ezrachi and Stucke, 2016; Lambrecht and Tucker, 2018), especially in the absence of clear liability rules (Galasso and Luo, 2018). This concept is not new (see Deary, 2001; Gardner, 1983; Wang, 2007; Winkless and Browning, 1978), and some work has been done in this field but it is more reactive than proactive (Vladeck, 2014). Some work already done in this area includes the EU RoboLaw Regulating Emerging Robotic Technologies in Europe: Robotics Facing Law and Ethics (2012), the EU (2014) Guidelines on Regulating Robotics, and Hosanagar's Algorithmic Bill of Rights (2019). Most of the existing laws assume AI is the servant to the human/organization and hence the human/organization should still be liable (read work by Čerka, Grigienė, and Sirbikytė, 2015).

At a government level, AI brings with it further opportunities for regulation, ensuring employment, and preventing inequality. What are the future regulations that may explode with respect to data privacy, civil rights, or as an outcome of lawsuits? An effort was made with respect to the ASILOMAR AI Principles. The State of California adopted the principles on September 7, 2018.[1] Many workshops and think tanks discussed similar topics.[2] The recent unrests in Google and Microsoft, where employees have voiced uncertainty of their organizations' commitment to defense contracts, make the question of the overarching values one that needs a clear definition. This unrest suggests that AI activities should be ideally based in a location that minimizes liabilities and facilitates open exploration and debate on AI.

The change in the EU regulations concerning data privacy (GDPR) hit small and medium-sized organizations harder than the large companies that had the funds to manage the cosmetic changes in some cases, the legal process and paying fines. This law resulted in less capital being raised in the EU versus the United States and the volumes of deals fell (Jia et al., 2018). At the scale AI is capable of, regulations may be an afterthought, and the policymakers need to understand the implications for organizations at scale may harm startups unless sufficient resources are provided for development through grants. The deeper the understanding of your potential export markets (countries and industries), the easier it gets to understand the legal implications.

## Management Level: Success Factors

Once the policy-level decisions are considered and outlined, you could move to the next phase considered critical: how do you manage AI-tech clusters? Here you need to focus on four success factors: anchor tenants, entrepreneurial culture, access to resources, and knowledge exchange and spillovers. Though impact and control are essential from a management point of view it is highlighted under a separate section only because of its importance.

### *The anchor tenant question*

Clusters act as a signal for future types of businesses that can thrive in the region (Romanelli and Khessina, 2005). The most compelling reason for future growth is the initial collaborators or anchor tenants (Brun and Jolley, 2011). Looking at the global semiconductor and ICT industry, clusters emerged from anchor tenants in fields like military, lighting engineering, or the radio-telecommunication sector. For example, in Israel the military served as the anchor tenant along with Technion (the Israeli Institute of Technology). In Silicon Valley, it was the Fairchild Conductors along with Stanford University and UC Berkeley (Scott and Kirst, 2017). So each industry embedded in the cluster ideally needs an anchor tenant, with significant R&D investments that can encourage smaller startups to get associated with the larger organization, which may come from the public or private sector.

The most prominent high-tech clusters are based near academic institutions or large research centers in large metros (e.g., see, Cooke and Huggins, 2018; Ketels and Memedovic, 2008). Clusters should have access to talent, finance, and inspiration (focusing on problem-solving). The proximity of universities or cities ideally should give the cluster a high density of populations (talent) and firms (specialist firms or be allied industries, services, etc., that feed into each other). A study of patents and research papers in metropolitan areas finds that there should be colocation of industrial R&D (anchor institutions), with upstream university research in cities resulting in vertical spillovers (Agarwal and Cockburn, 2003).

Surprisingly, when analyzing the AI national strategies, many countries do not identify anchor tenants (as existing commercial organizations). In Europe, there is a tendency to use nonprofits, research centers, and academic institutions. Canada was one of the few countries that identified regions of focus.

Complementaries are industries in the vertical and horizontal supply chain that can thrive off each other creating a healthy ecosystem (Porter, 1998: 78). Employees may job hop often between sectors, encouraging the transfer of knowledge (Fallick et al., 2006). Because early adopters are close to three times as likely to have a strategic roadmap for AI implementation, have clear governance models, know required employee skills, and have managed to find ways to control interoperability between legacy systems and new tech and identified cybersecurity threats (BCG, 2018), they are critical for a cluster. Opportunities are plenty and lie in crossroads of many traditional industries. When considering sustainability issues, e-waste and materials science will become a potential area of development. Because AI is more than just software or the service economy, and more and more it is being embedded into hardware across industries, an AI cluster perhaps maybe most effective at the component or sensor level.

### The entrepreneurial culture question

AI clusters survive where there is sharing of some information and spillover of diverse ideas, talents, and knowledge. OECD highlights encouraging entrepreneurship as the single most important reason for good practices for clusters (Potter and Miranda, 2009). This risk-taking attitude is one that will help us pivot (learning from failures), identify the right business opportunity, find talent that AI needs, and create the right system of human–AI teams (Thomas, 2019). Creating a cluster that can capture the entrepreneurial spirit requires careful planning (Stephens, 2019).

Technology entrepreneurs are most likely to contribute to a vibrant ecosystem (Endeavour Insights, 2014; Feldman et al., 2005). Many successful startup founders become angel investors, and this is needed to bring in venture capital and private equity funding for scaling enterprises. Venture capital has been linked to the success and transformation of clusters (Avnimelech and Teubal, 2006; Powell et al., 2002). One study finds that

US$ 1 in venture capital investment generates 3.1 times the number of patents compared to US$ 1 investment in R&D in traditional enterprises (Kortum and Lerner, 2000).

## The infrastructure and key resource question

There are three circles of infrastructure needs: the first is supporting services and facilities (accelerators, research, creative hubs); the second is public facilities like parks, retail, homes, and buildings; and the third will be networking facilities/infrastructure to encourage the act of networking (Baily and Montalbano, 2017; Stephens et al., 2019). The most vibrant clusters are not isolated but creep into residential areas and university pockets. Here the debate is the quality of life—access to a good standard of living, medical and educational facilities, commute time, and safety.

The inputs and outputs required to make a thriving AI cluster are data, skills or talent, hardware, software, and services. Data and human, technical skills will make the final product, which may be combinations of hardware, software, and ingenuity that could be exported or consumed as a product and services. Data volume is critical as it could improve the quality of AI decision-making, making it a competitive resource (Goldfarb and Trefler, 2018), and this may require cluster managers to encourage organizations to look at economies of scope, a variety of applications, or data sharing (Goldfarb and Trefler, 2018). Access to infrastructure and essential goods and services for production and export may be vital to the success of the firm (Westhead and Batstone, 1998; Porter, 1998). Among the many services, one of the most important is legal services. Legal services may take the form of protecting IP or understanding employee contracts. In knowledge-intensive sectors, highly skilled employees are known to go job hopping, and IT cluster bleeds into other sectors (Falick et al., 2006), which may be positive for the overall economy.

Capital becomes an essential resource (Porter, 1998; Häussler and Zademach, 2007). R&D and testing of AI maybe cost intensive. Government-subsidized or -funded labs are one way to ensure that there is some knowledge sharing. R&D centers in the United States may be more expensive than in the developing world, and governments may need to think of how they subsidize these costs to attract firms (De Fontenay and Erran, 2004). Access to research grants is one method to subsidize the cost of R&D. For example, EU Horizon 2020 seeds projects that can be commercialized. The ability to attract FDI may be another method to attract resources (see the Ireland case, Green, 2000). However, for a cluster to survive, there needs to be a minimum number of local firms over just foreign firms (Birkinshaw, 2000).

*The information and knowledge exchange and spillover question*

The OECD (2017) identifies networking as the second most important reason for cluster best practices. Access to information or data alone is not enough if there is no inherent ability to exchange knowledge (Tallman et al., 2004) and more importantly create new knowledge (Pouder and St. John, 1996; Saxenian, 1994). Only a part of new knowledge is technology. Networking can take the form of formal and informal networks through people movement, and planners need to consider urban setting (De Fontenay and Erran, 2004; Stephens, 2019). Networking needs to be within the cluster and outside (Li et al., 2013).

Israeli ICT companies are able to list on US stock markets and get acquired by leading US companies, which contributes to the competitiveness of the cluster (De Fontenay and Erran, 2004). The government can create knowledge- and resource-sharing platforms that facilitate interactions with supply chain, new markets, and academia (Lai et al., 2014). It has been found that tech- nology spillovers are critical for the development of high-technology clusters (Tallman et al., 2004). Research on AI international diffusion suggests that it is still rather weak and still resides in the location of the developer, provided the conditions are optimal, especially concerning data collection and public R&D investments (Goldfarb and Daniel, 2018; Fujii and Managi, 2018).

## Impact and Control Level: Bounded Reliability

Though the last set of decision, impact and control level is no less important as management and governance overlap, especially as AI falls in many gray areas of ethics. Hopefully, the ethics side of decision is considered in the first phase, but the fast-paced evolution of AI makes this an area of constant monitoring. Clusters grow organically and hence by tracking the success of the cluster, interventions can be planned to encourage the direction of growth and to ensure that the values and governance criteria important for the country or the cluster are embedded in the strategy inventions. Below is a checklist of a series of protocols that must be answered to ensure that the AI-tech cluster is optimized (Table 8.2). These questions have been grouped into seven themes— relevance to the region or country; scale planned; ethical framework; anchor tenants; entrepreneurial culture; infrastructure and resources; and informa- tion and knowledge spillover.

## Feedback Level: Agile Learning

The unique nature of the multidisciplinary convergence of AI technology demands a feedback loop for dynamic evolution from within. Since clusters

**Table 8.2** AI-tech clusters—overarching policy and management decisions

| Relevance | • Do you have a country/city citizen first approach? If you do, in what perspective should this be considered—base resources, talent, customer, head offices, production? What available country resources will you leverage to your advantage?<br>• What are the net jobs created versus net jobs destroyed?<br>• What is the domain of the AI cluster that will give you a competitive advantage? What is the cluster's core competency to start with?<br>• Can the cluster aggregate demand and lobbying for places/countries with similar needs? |
|---|---|
| Scale | • What is the probability of spillovers and how will you track this across government and private sectors where the technology can be embedded?<br>• What support can I give to help make the technology the dominant design and integrate it into multiple platforms and systems designing for interoperability or complementaries?<br>• What is net technology (hardware and software) imported versus net technology exported? |
| Ethics | • What are the sandboxing techniques already in place for experimentation for regulations? Is there a legislation experimentation policy?<br>• What are the values that drive the cluster?<br>• How would you provide support for patent protection, sharing of learnings from failure, cybersecurity, and a data collection system?<br>So AI has many concerns, especially when we are considering creating AI-tech zones or clusters. By understanding some of these challenges, AI clusters can be built to provide meaningful and well-thought-of innovations. Gone are the days when R&D worked in isolation to create new products. The scale of AI, the volumes of data, and the need for interoperability all make that a very obsolete concept. |
| Anchor tenants | • Who are the anchor tenants that can bring with them a threshold number of talents that can attract other tenants?<br>• What are the incentives that have been put in place to make this happen? Are the incentives beyond the cluster, including the quality of life? |

**Table 8.2** *(Cont.)*

| The entrepreneurial culture | • Is the regulatory environment and incentives in place to encourage entrepreneurship?<br>• Where is the young talent coming from (are there services to support young talent?)<br>• Where can they test? Also, is failure an option (are the rules and regulations supporting failure—like a bankruptcy law?) |
|---|---|
| Infrastructure and key resources | • What is the existing infrastructure the cluster will provide/incentivize, and what have they planned to develop? |
| Information and knowledge spillover | • What is the citizen contribution to intellectual capital versus the emphasis to attract world-class talent and keep them there?<br>Knowledge spillover is dependent on culture and the regulatory environment, but a healthy competitive ecosystem has high levels of mentorship and positive support for talent.<br>More important in the development of AI clusters is sharing failures as this may prevent failures at scale. |

*Source*: Author.

grow organically, it is impossible to predict the level of industry fragmentation; or the disruptions and megatrends that will disrupt the competitiveness of clusters. The conditions captured at the start of the development of a cluster may quickly become obsolete. The solution the above issues is to use the feedback loop to relook the policy and management-level decisions regularily. Agile learning is process driven, and Figure 8.2 shows key functions borrowed from knowledge management and software process models. It is defined as not only the ability to pick up new knowledge quickly and flexibly move on to different conclusions when warranted, it also involves not getting stuck in a particular point of view and being able to transfer lessons appropriately to new situations and experiences (DeRue et al., 2010). Agile learning is critical for AI-tech clusters.

## AI Boundary

In conclusion, an AI-tech cluster will be boundary spanning and eventually overlap with economics, residents' health, way of life, and culture. The pace of AI innovations requires AI-tech cluster managers to keep one step

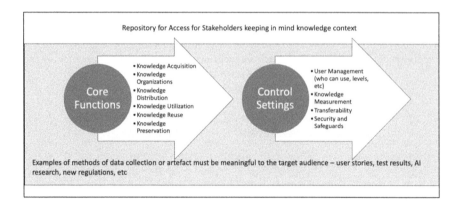

**Figure 8.2** Agile learning.
*Source*: Adapted from Amescua, Bermón, García, and Sanchez-Segura (2010).

ahead in policy regulations to support innovations, yet be mindful of possible regulations that prevent new tech from being misused. Boundary spanning requires market scanning and competing at an international level for new opportunities. This chapter is not exhaustive by any means as AI-tech clusters will overlap with entrepreneurial ecosystem, academia policies, regulatory environment, and quality of life, for example, and in that case you would need to look at knowledge spillovers and national competitiveness strategies.

## Notes

1    ACR-215 23 Asilomar AI Principles. http://leginfo.legislature.ca.gov/faces/billText Client.xhtml?bill_id=201720180ACR215.
2    https://futureoflife.org/ai-principles/.

## References

Agrawal, Ajay, and Iain Cockburn. "The anchor tenant hypothesis: Exploring the role of large, local, R&D-intensive firms in regional innovation systems." *International Journal of Industrial Organization* 21, no. 9 (2003): 1227–53.

Agrawal, Ajay, Joshua Gans, and Avi Goldfarb. "Economic policy for artificial intelligence." *Innovation Policy and the Economy* 19, no. 1 (2019): 139–59.

Amescua, Antonio, L. Bermón, J. García, and M.-I. Sanchez-Segura. "Knowledge repository to improve agile development processes learning." *IET Software* 4, no. 6 (2010): 434–44.

Avnimelech, Gil, and Morris Teubal. "Creating venture capital industries that co-evolve with high tech: Insights from an extended industry life cycle perspective of the Israeli experience." *Research Policy* 35, no. 10 (2006): 1477–98.

Baily, Martin Neil, and Nicholas Montalbano. *Clusters and Innovation Districts: Lessons from the United States Experience.* Washington, DC: Brookings Institution, 2017.

BCG. *AI in the Factory of the Future,* 2018. Available: https://image-src.bcg.com/Images/ BCG-AI-in-the-Factory-of-the-Future-Apr-2018_tcm9-188726.pdf.

Birkinshaw, Julian. "Upgrading of industry clusters and foreign investment." *International Studies of Management & Organization* 30, no. 2 (2000): 93–113.

Brun, Lukas C., and G. Jason Jolley. "Increasing stakeholder participation in industry cluster identification." *Economic Development Quarterly* 25, no. 3 (2011): 211–20.

Čerka, Paulius, Jurgita Grigienė, and Gintarė Sirbikytė. "Liability for damages caused by artificial intelligence." *Computer Law & Security Review* 31, no. 3 (2015): 376–89.

Chesbrough, Henry. *Open Business Models: How to Thrive in the New Innovation Landscape.* Boston: Harvard Business Press, 2006.

Cockburn, I., R. Henderson, and S. Stern. "The Impact of Artificial Intelligence on Innovation." In Agrawal, G. and Goldfarb, A. (eds.), *The Economics of Artificial Intelligence: An Agenda.* Chicago: University of Chicago Press, 2018.

Cooke, Philip, and Robert Huggins. "High-technology clustering in Cambridge (UK)." In Sforzi, Fabio (ed), In *The Institutions of Local Development,* pp. 51–74. Oxon: Routledge, 2018.

De Fontenay, Catherine and Erran Carmel. "Israel's Silicon Wadi: The forces behind cluster formation." In Bresnahan, Timothy (ed.), *Building High-tech Clusters: Silicon Valley and Beyond,* pp. 40–77. Cambridge: Cambridge University Press, 2004.

Deary, Ian J. "Human intelligence differences: A recent history." *Trends in Cognitive Sciences* 5, no. 3 (2001): 127–30.

DeRue, D. Scott, Susan J. Ashford, and Christopher G. Myers. "Learning agility: In search of conceptual clarity and theoretical grounding." *Industrial and Organizational Psychology* 5, no. 3 (2012): 258–79.

Dutton, Tim. (2018), An Overview of National AI Strategies, *Medium,* dated June 28, 2019. Available: https://medium.com/politics-ai/an-overview-of-national-ai-strategies-2a70ec6edfd [Accessed March 17, 2019].

Endeavor Insights. How Did Silicon Valley Become Silicon Valley? Three Surprising Lessons for Other Cities and Regions, 2014. Available: https://issuu.com/endeavorglobal1/docs/hdsvbsv__final_.

EU. *D6.2 'Guidelines for Regulating Robotics.* 2014. Available: http://www.robolaw.eu.

EU RoboLaw Regulating Emerging Robotic Technologies in Europe. Robotics Facing Law and Ethics. Collaborative Project FP7 GA 289092, 2012. Available: http://www.robolaw.eu/RoboLaw_files/documents/RoboLaw_20121004_Brochure_final.pdf. [Accessed 10 March, 2019].

Ezrachi, Ariel, and Maurice E. Stucke. 'Virtual Competition" *Journal of European Competition Law & Practice,* 7, No. 9 (2016): 585–586.

Fallick, Bruce, Charles A. Fleischman, and James B. Rebitzer. "Job-hopping in Silicon Valley: Some evidence concerning the microfoundations of a high-technology cluster." *Review of Economics and Statistics* 88, no. 3 (2006): 472–81.

Feldman, Maryann P., and Johanna L. Francis. "Homegrown solutions: Fostering cluster formation." *Economic Development Quarterly* 18, no. 2 (2004): 127–37.

Feldman, Maryann, Johanna Francis, and Janet Bercovitz. "Creating a cluster while building a firm: Entrepreneurs and the formation of industrial clusters." *Regional Studies* 39, no. 1 (2005): 129–41.

Franklin, Stan. "A foundational architecture for artificial general intelligence." In Goertzel, Ben, and Wang, Pei (eds), *Advances in Artificial General Intelligence: Concepts, Architectures and Algorithms* 6 (2007): 36–54.

Franklin, Stan, and Art Graesser. "Is it an agent, or just a program?: A taxonomy for autonomous agents." In *International Workshop on Agent Theories, Architectures, and Languages*, pp. 21–35. Berlin: Springer, 1996.

Fujii, Hidemichi, and Shunsuke Managi. "Trends and priority shifts in artificial intelligence technology invention: A global patent analysis." *Economic Analysis and Policy* 58 (2018): 60–69.

Galasso, Alberto, and Hong Luo. "Punishing Robots: issues in the economics of tort liability and innovation in artificial intelligence." *The Economics of Artificial Intelligence: An Agenda*, pp. 493–504. Chicago: University of Chicago Press, 2018.

Gardner, Howard. *Frames of Mind*. New York: Basic Books, 1983.

Gardner, Howard. *Frames of Mind: The Theory of Multiple Intelligences*. New York: Basic Books, 2011.

Goertzel, Ben, and Cassio Pennachin. "Contemporary approaches to artificial general intelligence." In Goertzel, Ben and Pennachin, Cassio (eds.), *Artificial General Intelligence*, pp. 1–30. Berlin: Springer, 2007.

Goldfarb, Avi, and Daniel Trefler. "AI and international trade." In Ajay Agrawal, Joshua Gans, and Avi Goldfarb (eds.), *The Economics of Artificial Intelligence: An Agenda*, pp. 463–449. Chicago: University of Chicago Press, 2018.

Green, Roy. "Irish ICT cluster." In *Paper delivered to the OECD Cluster Focus Group Workshop*, Utrecht, 2000.

Hall, Peter. *Cities of Tomorrow: An Intellectual History of Urban Planning and Design since 1880*. West Sussex: John Wiley, 2014.

Häussler, Carolin, and Hans-Martin Zademach. "Cluster performance reconsidered: Structure, linkages, and paths in the German biotechnology industry, 1996–2003." *Schmalenbach Business Review* 59, no. 3 (2007): 261–81.

Herzing, Denise L. "Profiling nonhuman intelligence: An exercise in developing unbiased tools for describing other 'types' of intelligence on earth." *Acta Astronautica* 94, no. 2 (2014): 676–80.

Hosanagar, K. *A Human Guide to Machine Intelligence—How Algorithms Are Shaping Our Lives and How We Can Stay in Control*. New York: Viking, 2019.

India. National Strategy for Artificial Intelligence, NITI Aayog, 2018.

Jia, Jian, Ginger Zhe Jin, and Liad Wagman. The Short-Run Effects of GDPR on Technology Venture Investment, 2018. Available: https://papers.ssrn.com/sol3/papers.cfm?abstract_id=3278912 [Accessed February 16, 2019].

Katz, Jerome. A., Scott R. Safranski, and Omar Khan. (2003). "Virtual instant global entrepreneurship." *Journal of International Entrepreneurship* 1, no. 1: 43–57.

Ketels, Christian H. M., and Olga Memedovic. "From clusters to cluster-based economic development." *International Journal of Technological Learning, Innovation and Development* 1, no. 3 (2008): 375–92.

Kortum, Samuel, and Josh Lerner. "Assessing the contribution of venture capital to innovation." *RAND Journal of Economics* (2000): 674–692.

Kortum, Samuel, and Josh Lerner. "Does venture capital spur innovation?" In Libecap, Gary D. *Entrepreneurial Inputs and Outcomes: New Studies of Entrepreneurship in the United States*, pp. 1–44. Bingley: Emerald Group, 2001.

Küpper, Daniel, Marcus Lorenz, Kristain Kuhlmann, Olivier Bouffault, Yew Heng Lim, Jonathan Van Wyck, Sebastian Köcher, and Jan Schlageter. *AI in the Factory of the Future.* BCG, dated April 18, 2018. Available: https://www.bcg.com/publications/2018/artificial-intelligence-factory-future.aspx [Accessed February 22, 2019].

Lai, Yung-Lung, Maw-Shin Hsu, Feng-Jyh Lin, Yi-Min Chen, and Yi-Hsin Lin. "The effects of industry cluster knowledge management on innovation performance." *Journal of Business Research* 67, no. 5 (2014): 734–39.

Lambrecht, Anja, Catherine Tucker, and Caroline Wiertz. "Advertising to early trend propagators: Evidence from twitter." *Marketing Science* 37, no. 2 (2018): 177–199.

Li, Wan, Rajaram Veliyath, and Justin Tan. "Network characteristics and firm performance: An examination of the relationships in the context of a cluster." *Journal of Small Business Management* 51, no. 1 (2013): 1–22.

Malmberg, Anders, Örjan Sölvell, and Ivo Zander. "Spatial clustering, local accumulation of knowledge, and firm competitiveness." *Geografiska Annaler: Series B, Human Geography* 78, no. 2 (1996): 85–97.

Maturana, Humberto R. "The organization of the living: A theory of the living organization." *International Journal of Man-Machine Studies* 7, no. 3 (1975): 313–32.

McCarthy, John. "From here to human-level AI." *Artificial Intelligence* 171, no. 18 (2007): 1174–82.

Ng, Andrew. *Introduction to Artificial Intelligence.* Coursera, 2019. Available: https://www.coursera.org/learn/ai-for-everyone?

OECD. Enhancing the Contributions of SMEs in a Global and Digitalised Economy, Paris, 2017.

Pennachin, Cassio and Ben Goertzel. "Contemporary Approaches to Artificial General Intelligence". In Goertzel, Ben and Pennachin, Cassio (eds.), *Artificial General Intelligence*, pp. 1–28. New York: Springer, 2007.

Porter, Michael E. "The Technological Dimension of Competitive Strategy", in: R. Rosenbloom (ed.), *Research on Technological Innovation, Management and Policy*, Vol. 1, pp. 1–34. Greenwich CT: JAI Press, Inc., 1983.

Porter, Michael E. *Clusters and the New Economics of Competition*, Boston, MA: Harvard Business School Press, 1998.

Potter, Jonathan, and Gabriella Miranda. Clusters, Innovations & Entrepreneurship, (2009, OECD). Available: https://dx.doi.org/10.1787/9789264044326-en. [Accessed March 1, 2019].

Pouder, Richard, and Caron H. St. John. "Hot spots and blind spots: Geographical clusters of firms and innovation." *Academy of Management Review* 21, no. 4 (1996): 1192–225.

Powell, Walter W., Kenneth W. Koput, James I. Bowie, and Laurel Smith-Doerr. "The spatial clustering of science and capital: Accounting for biotech firm-venture capital relationships." *Regional Studies* 36, no. 3 (2002): 291–305.

Romanelli, Elaine, and Olga M. Khessina. "Regional industrial identity: Cluster configurations and economic development." *Organization Science* 16, no. 4 (2005): 344–58.

Saxenian, Annalee. *Regional Advantage: Culture and Competition in Silicon Valley and Route 128.* Cambridge, MA: Harvard University Press, 1994.

Scott, W. Richard, and Michael W. Kirst. *Higher Education and Silicon Valley: Connected but Conflicted.* Baltimore, MD: John Hopkins University Press, 2017.

Stephens, Melodena. "Cities as custodians for entrepreneurial opportunity." In Iftikhar, M. N., Justice J., and Audretsch, D. (eds.), *Urban Studies and Entrepreneurship.* pp. 31–49 Switzerland: Springer International AG, 2019.

Stephens, M., I. A. Moonesar, M. El Sholkamy, and Awamleh, R. *Future Governments*. UK Bingley: Emerald Group, 2019.

Strohmeier, Stefan, and Franca Piazza. "Artificial intelligence techniques in human resource management—A conceptual exploration." In Kahraman, Cengiz and Onar, Sezi Cevik (eds.), *Intelligent Techniques in Engineering Management*, pp. 149–72. Cham: Springer, 2015.

Tallman, Stephen, Mark Jenkins, Nick Henry, and Steven Pinch. "Knowledge, clusters, and competitive advantage." *Academy of Management Review* 29, no. 2 (2004): 258–71.

Thomas, R. Commentary—AI Is Not Magic—It's Time to Demystify and Apply, Information Week, dated February 21, 2019. Available: https://www.informationweek.com/big-data/ai-machine-learning/ai-is-not-magic---its-time-to-demystify-and-apply/a/d-id/1333930?linkId=64045036 [Accessed February 26, 2019].

Vladeck, David C. "Machines without principals: Liability rules and artificial intelligence." *Washington Law Review* 89 (2014): 117.

Wang, Pei. "The logic of intelligence." In Goertzel, Ben and Pennachin, Cassio (eds.), *Cognitive Technologies in Cognitive Technologies*, pp. 31–60. Heidelberg: Springer, 2007.

Wang, Yingxu. "On abstract intelligence: Toward a unifying theory of natural, artificial, machinable, and computational intelligence." *International Journal of Software Science and Computational Intelligence (IJSSCI)* 1, no. 1 (2009): 1–17.

Westhead, Paul, and Stephen Batstone. "Independent technology-based firms: The perceived benefits of a science park location." *Urban Studies* 35, no. 12 (1998): 2197–219.

Winkless, Nels, and Iben Browning. *Robots on your Doorstep (A Book about Thinking Machines)*. Robotics Press, 1978.

# Part III

# AI AND THE ENHANCEMENT OF GOVERNANCE

# Chapter 9

# AI-GOVERNMENT VERSUS E-GOVERNMENT: HOW TO REINVENT GOVERNMENT WITH AI?

## Al Naqvi

### The Next Phase or a New Revolution

Is AI-government more, or different, than the e-government? Since the inception of the Internet, scholars and practitioners have advocated the use of Internet in government. Commonly known as e-government, the concept materialized over several decades and we have seen various manifestations of that in different times and in different countries. In the early stages of the Internet revolution, scholars recognized that the transformational success of e-business has a role to play in government and identified some exciting features of e-government. It was clarified that e-government involves using technology to benefit citizens; it is about providing seamless and integrated service to citizens and building a partnership between government and citizens (Fang, 2002; Silcock, 2001). It was recognized that various configurations of relationships such as G2C, C2G, and G2G are possible (C is citizen, and G is government) (Fang, 2002). It was viewed as a paradigm change when traditional bureaucracy will be replaced by collaboration and network building (Tat-kei Ho, 2002). It was also recognized that the impact will not just be on federal and state level but also at municipal, town, or city levels of government (Moon, 2002). In fact, the optimists viewed it as a global phenomenon (Jaeger and Thompson, 2003).

As citizen benefit became the underlying driver of e-government service development and design, at least three integrated challenges were identified (Jaeger and Bertot, 2010): (1) a theoretical framework needed to be developed that focused on the strategic imperative, high-level concepts, and value-centric transformation (Anthopoulos and Fitsilis, 2014); (2) a people-focused model needed to be in place to manage and educate the decision-makers, manage change, create awareness and a sense of urgency, and show how such a transformation will benefit citizens (Rowley, 2011; van Velsen et al., 2009; Wagner et al., 2016; Wassenaar, 2000); and (3) a technical design, process maps, infrastructure, analysis, interoperability, technology design, and implementation standards and approaches needed to be articulated and presented (Janssen and Veenstra, 2005; Pardo et al., 2012; van Velsen et al., 2009).

While e-government initiatives were still going on a new technological revolution has started (Makridakis, 2017). The important feature of this revolution is that it is not merely an extension of the "e" or "Internet" revolution (Schwab, 2015). It is not the next phase of the digital transformation. For one, the underlying technology is not based upon line-by-line code written to instruct the computer to do something. It is not deterministic and not accomplished with the formulaic accuracy that exists in normal computer programs. It is statistical in nature, based upon data science, and driven by training algorithms that learn to accomplish tasks. Second, its very nature lifts the restrictions imposed by the strict mechanical adherence to the specific set of instructions given to the machine. It is no longer constrained. It can accumulate experience, learn, and adapt. Third, the combination of processing power, data availability, and algorithms has unleashed a powerful way to develop and deploy these systems. Fourth, these systems are not bounded by the limited data types with neatly organized transactional data and instead can utilize unstructured data as well (e.g., sound, video, and other types of data). Fifth, the data being recorded is enormous and can be used to build machine learning-based intelligent automation (Qiu et al., 2016).

The above five factors demarcate the revolution from the previous technological stages and allocates to the new age of intelligent automation its own spatial boundary. This allocation of spatial boundary also signifies that the distance between it and the digital/e/Internet revolution is no less than the distance between digital/e/Internet revolution and the paper-based world in the pre-IT era—best described in the words of the author of *The Fourth Industrial Revolution*: "In its scale, scope and complexity, what I consider to be the fourth industrial revolution is unlike anything humankind has experienced before" (Schwab, 2016).

Once it is recognized that we have entered a new revolutionary time, we must realize that new demands are placed upon how we think and approach this revolution. Of course, it doesn't help if we are still dealing with the unresolved challenges and issues from the previous era.

**From E- to the AI-Government**

Clarifying what citizen centricity is can set the foundation for more discussion on AI. A citizen-friendly government provides services that citizens need and want, does it in the best possible way, and for the lowest cost possible. This obviously implies that the government mindset shifts from authoritarian administration to value creation for citizens (Flak et al., 2015). Value gets created when people's lives improve.

E-service and customer satisfaction are two different things. One could represent the technical delivery part of the service, for example, the user interface, the user satisfaction, the speed of screen loading with data, and so on. The other could be at a different level of abstraction where other quality-centric questions can be asked—such as whether the citizen benefited from the service, whether his or her rights and experience increased, whether the service was necessary for his or her protection, whether the service reduced the cost or time burden. Thus, having an automated service is one thing, delivering it with excellence another thing, and truly creating value for citizens yet another thing.

In the early stages of e-government conceptualization, Layne and Lee, (2001) envisioned a four-stage growth model composed of: (1) cataloging, (2) transaction, (3) vertical integration, and (4) horizontal integration. The simplicity of the model does a good job in capturing the systematic progression of the requisite capability buildup. In 2006, Andersen and Henriksen expanded the stage model and presented it as a maturity model that focused on bringing end users into perspective and also focusing on not what was technologically feasible but instead on what will be beneficial for the citizens regardless of its impact on internal dynamics (Andersen and Henriksen, 2006). A decade later after the Lyane and Lee model, Lee (2010) revisited and compared and contrasted the original model with several other stage models. The linearity and process orientation of the stage model had attracted several consulting firms and market research firms to develop their own models. In the review, Lee (2010) identified that the integration of two major dimensions of operations/technology perspective and citizen/service perspective defined a space where maturity of e-government models can materialize. By 2010, it was evident that technology alone is insufficient and emphasis on customer/citizen service is necessary (Gagliardi et al., 2017). Thus, a balanced approach was proposed where inward focus (i.e., technological capability) was integrated with the outward focus (citizen service needs and requirements) (Das et al., 2017). As both supply and demand sides of IT were clarified (Gauld et al., 2010), scholars recognized that benefits should not just be based upon quantitative factors but qualitative factors—such as empowerment, social cohesion, and self-esteem—should also be considered (Gomez and Pather, 2012).

The focus on technology without considering citizen needs was addressed as a problem. Evaluation paradigms were created to understand the performance of services. These frameworks, for example, the COBRA framework

(Cost, Benefit, Risk, and Opportunity) by Osman et al. (2014), demonstrated the growing emphasis on understanding what services will be accepted, preferred, needed, and adopted by various stakeholders. Chen (2010) outlined the importance of citizen-centric government—declaring, in accordance with United Nations, that the ideal manifestation of e-government is indeed citizen-centric government.

Chun et al. (2018) made a distinction between Government 1.0 (the web presence, interaction, and transactional stages) and Government 2.0, which they described as "when the government promotes shared governance to transform how the government operates, in terms of seamless information flow and collaborative decision making." This was presented as the next step in the evolution of e-government. Cocreation of value by multiple stakeholders became the next evolution of the base paradigms (Flak et al., 2015).

Building upon the previous developments, scholars began focusing on "smartness" in government. It was not just about e-government anymore, the next evolutionary step was to create a smart government. Gil-Garcia et al. (2016) identified 14 dimensions of what makes a government smart, and the dimensions included factors such as innovation based, resiliency, and so on. But smartness was not necessarily linked to AI. A smart government could have been smart simply based upon nonintelligent systems. The term "smart" in that connotation did not imply intelligence of systems but the concept that technology can enable multiple dimensions of desirable capabilities that empower humans, and when it is designed and implemented to achieve those dimensions, smartness results. In other words, intelligence was not viewed as a necessary attribute of technology as much as it was seen as something whose use made humans smarter.

By 2017 though, there was clear recognition that big data and data itself can be major sources of innovation and modernization. For example, claims were made that BOLD, Big, and Open-Linked Data can lead to "dramatic transformation of public sector systems and can create societal benefits" (Janssen et al., 2017). What was missed, however, is that the conceptual shift from viewing systems solely as line-by-line instruction-based programmed code to *data-centric and data-driven systems* constitutes a fundamental change in our understanding of both technology and citizen services—the two core dimensions of e-government. Data-driven systems are not applications that capture some elements of reality (e.g., transactions, temperature, logistics, etc.) and then generate reports on them via some analytical engines (e.g., business intelligence, business analytics). They are systems that result from the data being transformed into functions that model the reality that is represented in the data, and therefore embedding the ability to display intelligence (Qiu et al., 2016). That reality could be known or unknown to humans. When the reality is known, the discovery of the representative function of the data is known as supervised learning. When only the inputs are known and it is expected that some relationship between the inputs could reveal outputs of interest, it is known as unsupervised learning. The revelations from machine learning-based systems could be extraordinary, and in some cases all humans can do is to observe the outputs and inputs without necessarily understanding the underlying logic or mechanics of why a machine is making a recommendation or classifying something into a category (Gordon-Murnane, 2018).

Data-centric systems and predictive modeling take us into the territory of AI (Ghahramani, 2015). Machine learning—that is, teaching machines to perform cognitive tasks that are typically performed by humans—is made possible by having large volumes of data and the ability to process it. Training algorithms to learn to perform tasks is becoming the fundamental driver of value. The concept of automation itself transitioned from automation achieved via machines that are completely subservient to human commands and the machines that can learn, accumulate experience, and adapt, leading to the introduction of new competitive dynamics (Naqvi, 2017).

The emergence of the intelligent systems is too revolutionary to be confined to the digital-era e-government. It is a fundamental shift and hence constitutes its own body of knowledge and is captured by the term "AI-government."

The uniqueness of this paradigm can be appreciated by recognizing that unlike in the e-government frameworks where systems and stakeholders were separated, in AI-government it is necessary to lose that distinction. The systems can act as stakeholders. The link between human cognitive apparatus and the intelligent system could become a two-way influencer where humans don't just passively absorb information based on their needs and wants, but the intelligent system can influence human cognition by exposing and rup-turing the shields through which we process information. Learning can be accelerated, decelerated, modified, and manipulated. Human actions can be both influenced and controlled. Human life can be both benefited and harmed. Intelligence, therefore, is not interactive in the sense the word "inter-active" has been used in IT (i.e., provides interaction to human based upon limited and predetermined responses) but instead becomes interactive as when we consider the interaction when two or more humans talk to each other.

## Model of AI-Government

The AI-government is a government that uses the intellect and physical cap-abilities of machines to serve citizens. In this case, machines can be viewed as physical or digital manifestations of artifacts that can resolve uncertainty on their own. To simplify the discussion, these artifacts can be termed as "bots."

The bots necessarily act with the environment in which they operate, and the environment is composed of other systems, humans, and the physical or digital world (Russell and Norvig, 1994). A bot's environment can be as simple as a transactional data file coming into the bot or as complex as multidimensional, unstructured data read by advanced sensors of a robot.

In the current state of technology, the bots are being trained to perform specific tasks and, when combined with other bots, can perform more complex tasks. We can have tasks as simple as updating data in respective fields on a screen or as complex as processing and deciding on a mortgage application. The combination of bots with other bots produces more complex systems such as the autonomous car or a new drug development system.

Without evoking the debate about the power dynamics between government and citizens and when considered purely in the technological terms, the ultimate purpose of the AI-government can be to create an integrated autonomous system that can provide effective governance and establish social order without any human intervention. This implies that we can envision a world where all government services are provided with intelligent systems or bots—thus eliminating the need for any human intervention in running or managing the government. While such a lofty goal can seem far-fetched, what it does do is to enable us to define a ground floor for the AI-government and probably even build some additional floors to solidify the early stage of the AI-revolution.

Our desire to build such cognitive capabilities could be driven by our government or agency's normal functional goals to cut costs, reduce waste, or improve service. However, approaching intelligent automation from such goals does not do justice to the potential of the AI-government.

First, while focusing on cost cutting or service improvement, we may ignore that AI-centric process automation may not simply be the automation of the current human-centric process. As Noam Chomsky once responded to the question "Can machines be intelligent?" by answering with a question "Can submarines swim?" we need to understand that the intelligent machine-centric process can be widely different than our normal human-centric processes (Araki, 2018). The cognitive revolution framework is facilitating the convergence of brain, mind, and machines (Gershman et al., 2015), creating a new type of rationality. The entire digital revolution automation was built with human at the center of the technology. It wasn't designed for human-less automation. Our ability to rethink process management from a machine–human perspective is critical to embracing the AI-revolution. That is why the IEEE recognized the need to offer terms and concepts in intelligent automation (IEEE Corporate Advisory Group (CAG), 2017) as distinct from normal automation.

Second, the process when designed for human consumption, involvement, and supervision was necessarily less effective than the process designed for combined machine and human consumption. In other words, machines can be on both ends, of providing a citizen service and of receiving a citizen service on behalf of the citizen. For instance, a personal tax management bot in the service of a human (citizen) can communicate with a taxation bot (government) to find answers to specific questions.

Designing services for AI-government model has at least three parts—intelligence, governance, and service quality.

### *Intelligence*

Intelligence implies that the bots employed to perform services exhibit intelligent behavior—which on the lower end could simply be the automation of basic digital processes as delivered by Robotic Process Automation (van der Aalst et al., 2018) and on the higher end could be the deployment of advanced machine learning-enabled learning systems that use supervised, unsupervised, and reinforcement learning to perform various intelligent tasks (Li, 2018). Their learning behavior is not only manifested in the digital world but is also embedded within the physical or mechanical systems such as advanced robots, drones, and autonomous cars. The bots can display collaborative behavior with each other in a swarm or subset of swarm—or simply in a multiagent system (Aydin and Fellows, 2017). The collaborative behavior can also result from machine–human interaction or human–robot collaboration (Wang and Zhang, 2017). Designing services in this paradigm implies understanding the performance criteria of the bot. One approach to use is the SADAL® system to divide the task of service development of intelligent agent into Sense, Analyze, Decide, Act, and Learn (Naqvi, 2017). Here are some design features for designing AI-government services:

- *Intelligent Performance:* Intelligently designed services not only perform but as they perform, their performance improves.
- *Intelligent Behavior:* Intelligent machines display intelligent behavior and therefore can have a direct interaction with human mind. This means they can possess the ability to influence, understand behavior, discover what humans are intentionally or unintentionally hiding, and create intelligent interaction as happens between two or more humans.
- *Intelligent Design:* Intelligent services are not just a better replica of existing services. Instead they are designed anew and with multiple goals.
- *Intelligent Access:* Intelligent access implies that all who want to use the service can access it and, in some cases, service goes to the users versus the other way.

- *Intelligent Architecture*: Intelligent architecture is a multientity, multiagent system that can have both physical and digital manifestations. The architecture is approached not from a single service design perspective but instead from a broad infrastructure that can enable the creation and provision of various services.

### Governance

Trust was always an integral consideration in e-government (Alzahrani et al., 2017; Tolbert and Mossberger, 2006). Trust is also one of the most critical issues. (Hengstler et al., 2016; Hoff and Bashir, 2015; Parasuraman and Manzey, 2010). Unlike nonintelligent machines where governance implies governing the behavior of the operator of the machine, for example, driver of a car, pilot of an airplane, or a computer programmer, the governance of intelligent systems requires governing both systems and operators. Intelligent systems can learn and adopt. Their learning can be biased, conditioned upon the data used to train them (Gordon-Murnane, 2018; Potapov and Rodionov, 2014; van Otterlo, 2018). The interaction of multiple bots can form a complex system, and complex systems can display unpredictable behaviors due to emergence (Heylighen and Lenartowicz, 2016). Governance implies that the artifacts deployed in AI-government are safe (i.e., perform in accordance with what they are supposed to do and do nothing else) and stable (i.e., their performance can reliably persist over their life).

### Service quality

The third necessary component is that service being delivered by the AI-government must fulfill the quality standards. Quality in this case is not limited to what has been previously identified as critical for e-government (Janita and Miranda, 2018; Karunasena and Deng, 2012; Papadomichelaki and Mentzas, 2012; Rana and Dwivedi, 2015; Sá et al., 2017) but must also include the ability of the artifact to improve itself. The ability to improve itself is greatly dependent upon the artifact following more predictable evolutionary paths. The service quality can quickly deteriorate when a service artifact's learning deviates from its goals or when the interaction between multiple artifacts creates unnecessary or unanticipated problems.

### Conclusion

AI-government is vastly different than e-government. As governments embrace AI-based technologies, they must consider adopting the AI-government model.

Without such adoption they will stay paralyzed between the past and the future (Gauld et al., 2010; Stefanovic et al., 2016). It has happened before—when governments attempted to embrace the e-government models and their inability to fully comprehend that a paradigm change had happened created massive project failures (Gomez and Pather, 2012; Rose and Grant, 2010). However, the adoption of the AI-government model requires a completely different thinking than what we are used to. The intellectualization of technology is not a simple evolutionary step. It is a revolution of its own. Designing services should not be approached as in the past and new methods and creative thinking will be needed to develop service vision (Carlsen et al., 2014). Safety in any type of human and bot interaction will be critical (Wang and Zhang, 2017). Impact of cognitive machines on both citizens and organizations needs to be included in design considerations (Nobre, 2014; Nobre et al., 2009). Governance and bias management are key design issues. Managing quality will be critical as systems will display evolutionary characteristic. Further research on formalizing the AI-government quality requirements, governance requirements, and design methodologies will help accelerate and propel governments to embrace the new revolution efficiently and effectively.

## References

van der Aalst, W. M. P., Bichler, Martin and Heinzl, Armin (2018) Robotic process automation. *Business and Information Systems Engineering* [online] 60 (4), 269–72. Available from: https://doi.org/10.1007/s12599-018-0542-4.

Alzahrani, L., Al-Karaghouli, Wafi, and Weerakkody, Vishanth (2017) Analysing the critical factors influencing trust in e-government adoption from citizens' perspective: A systematic review and a conceptual framework. *International Business Review* [online] 26 (1), 164–75.

Andersen, K. V. and Henriksen, H. Z. (2006) E-government maturity models: Extension of the Layne and Lee model. *Government Information Quarterly* [online] 23 (2), 236–48.

Anthopoulos, L. and Fitsilis, P. (2014) Trends in e-strategic management. *International Journal of Public Administration in the Digital Age* [online] 1 (1), 15–38.

Araki, N. (2018) Alan Turing's Question. *Bull. Hiroshima Inst. Tech. Research* 52 33–42.

Aydin, M. E., and Fellows, R. (2017) *A Reinforcement Learning Algorithm for Building Collaboration in Multi-agent systems* [online]. Available from: http://arxiv.org/abs/1711.10574.

Carlsen, H., Johansson, Linda, Wikman-Svahn, Per, and Dreborg, Karl Henrik (2014) Co-evolutionary scenarios for creative prototyping of future robot systems for civil protection. *Technological Forecasting and Social Change* [online] 84, 93–100. Available from: http://dx.doi.org/10.1016/j.techfore.2013.07.016.

Chen, Y. C. (2010) Citizen-centric E-government services: Understanding integrated citizen service information systems. *Social Science Computer Review* [online] 28 (4), 427–42.

Chun, S. A., Shulman, Stuart, Sandoval, Rodrigo, and Hovy, Eduard (2018) Government 2.0: Making connections between citizens, data and government. *Information Polity* [online] 15 (1,2), 1–9.

Das, A., Singh, Harminder, and Joseph, Damien (2017) A longitudinal study of e-government maturity. *Information and Management* [online] 54 (4), 415–26. Available from: http://dx.doi.org/10.1016/j.im.2016.09.006.

Fang, Z. (2002) E-government in digital era: Concept, practice, and development. *The Internet and Management* 10 (2), 1–22. Available from: http://citeseerx.ist.psu.edu/viewdoc/download?doi=10.1.1.133.9080&rep=rep1&type=pdf.

Flak, L. S., Solli-Saether, Hans, and Straub, Detmar (2015) Towards a theoretical model for co-realization of IT value in government. *Proceedings of the Annual Hawaii International Conference on System Sciences* [online] (March 2015), 2486–494.

Gagliardi, D., Schina, Laura, Sarcinella, Marco Lucio, Mangialardi, Giovanna, Niglia, Francesco, and Corallo, Angelo (2017) Information and communication technologies and public participation: Interactive maps and value added for citizens. *Government Information Quarterly* [online] 34 (1), 153–66. Available from: https://doi.org/10.1016/j.giq.2016.09.002.

Gauld, R., Goldfinch, Shaun, and Horsburgh, Simon (2010) Do they want it? Do they use it? The "Demand-Side" of e-Government in Australia and New Zealand. *Government Information Quarterly* [online] 27 (2), 177–86.

Gershman, S. J., Horvitz, Eric J., and Tenenbaum, Joshua B. (2015) Computational rationality: A converging paradigm for intelligence in brains, minds, and machines. *Science* [online] 349 (6245), 273–78.

Ghahramani, Z. (2015) Probabilistic machine learning and artificial intelligence. *Nature* [online] 521 (7553), 452–59. Available from: http://dx.doi.org/10.1038/nature14541.

Gil-Garcia, J. R., Zhang, Jing, and Puron-Cid, Gabriel (2016) Conceptualizing smartness in government: An integrative and multi-dimensional view. *Government Information Quarterly* [online] 33 (3), 524–34. Available from: http://dx.doi.org/10.1016/j.giq.2016.03.002.

Gomez, R., and Pather, S. (2012) ICT evaluation: Are we asking the right questions? *Electronic Journal of Information Systems in Developing Countries* [online] 50 (1), 1–14.

Gordon-Murnane, L. (2018) Ethical, explainable artificial intelligence: Bias and principles. *Online Searcher* 42 (2), 22–44. Available from: http://search.ebscohost.com/login.aspx?direct=true&db=cin20&AN=128582745&site=ehost-live.

Hengstler, M., et al. (2016) Applied artificial intelligence and trust—The case of autonomous vehicles and medical assistance devices. *Technological Forecasting and Social Change* [online] 105, 105–20. Available from: http://dx.doi.org/10.1016/j.techfore.2015.12.014.

Heylighen, F., and Lenartowicz, M. (2016) The Global Brain as a model of the future information society: An introduction to the special issue. *Technological Forecasting and Social Change* [online] 114. Available from: http://www.sciencedirect.com/science/article/pii/S004016251630539X.

Hoff, K. A., and Bashir, M. (2015) Trust in automation: Integrating empirical evidence on factors that influence trust. *Human Factors* [online] 57 (3), 407–34.

IEEE Corporate Advisory Group (CAG) (2017) IEEE Guide for Terms and Concepts in Intelligent Process Automation. The Institute of Electrical and Electronics Engineers Standards Association, 1–16.

Jaeger, P. T., and Bertot, J. C. (2010) Designing, implementing, and evaluating user-centered and citizen-centered E-government. *International Journal of Electronic Government Research* 6 (2), 1–17.

Jaeger, P. T., and Thompson, K. M. (2003) E-government around the world: Lessons, challenges, and future directions. *Government Information Quarterly* [online] 20 (4), 389–94. Available from: https://linkinghub.elsevier.com/retrieve/pii/S0740624X03000789.

Janita, M. S., and Miranda, F. J. (2018) Quality in e-Government services: A proposal of dimensions from the perspective of public sector employees. *Telematics and Informatics* [online] 35 (2), 457–69. Available from: https://doi.org/10.1016/j.tele.2018.01.004.

Janssen, M., Anouze, Abdel Latef, Irani, Zahir, Al-Ayoubi, Baydaa, Lee, Habin, Balc, Asim, Medeni, Tunç D., and Weerakkody, Vishanth (2017) Driving public sector innovation using big and open linked data (BOLD). *Information Systems Frontiers* [online] 19 (2), 189–95.

Janssen, M., and van Veenstra, A. F. (2005) Stages of growth in e-government: An architectural approach. *Journal of e-Government* 3 (4), 193–200.

Karunasena, K., and Deng, H. (2012) Critical factors for evaluating the public value of e-government in Sri Lanka. *Government Information Quarterly* [online] 29 (1), 76–84. Available from: http://dx.doi.org/10.1016/j.giq.2011.04.005.

Layne, K., and Lee, J. (2001) Developing a fully functional e-government: A four stage model. *Government Information Quarterly* 18 (2), 122–38.

Lee, J. (2010) 10 year retrospect on stage models of e-Government: A qualitative meta-synthesis. *Government Information Quarterly* [online] 27 (3), 220–30. Available from: http://dx.doi.org/10.1016/j.giq.2009.12.009.

Li, Y. (2018) Deep reinforcement learning: An overview. *Lecture Notes in Networks and Systems* [online] 16, 426–40.

Makridakis, S. (2017) *Artificial Intelligence (AI) Revolution: Its Impact on Society and Firms.* Forthcoming.

Moon, J. M. (2002) The evolution of E-government among municipalities: Rhetoric or reality? *Public Administration Review* [online] 62 (4), 424–33.

Naqvi, A. (2017) Competitive dynamics of AI economy: The wicked problem of cognitive competition—June 2017. *Journal of Economics Library* 4 (2), 1–8.

Nobre, F. S., (2014) The roles of cognitive machines in customer-centric organizations. *Technological, Managerial and Organizational Core Competencies* [online] (January 2012), 653–74. Available from: http://services.igi-global.com/resolvedoi/resolve.aspx?doi=10.4018/978-1-61350-165-8.ch035.

Nobre, F. S., et al. (2009) The impact of cognitive machines on complex decisions and organizational change. *AI and Society* [online] 24 (4), 365–81.

Osman, I. H., Anouze, Abdel Latef, Irani, Zahir, Al-Ayoubi, Baydaa, Lee, Habin; Balc, Asim; Medeni, Tunç D., and Weerakkody, Vishanth (2014) COBRA framework to evaluate e-government services: A citizen-centric perspective. *Government Information Quarterly* [online] 31 (2), 243–56.

van Otterlo, M. (2018) *Gatekeeping Algorithms with Human Ethical Bias: The Ethics of Algorithms in Archives, Libraries and Society* (October 2017), 1–55. Available from: http://arxiv.org/abs/1801.01705.

Papadomichelaki, X., and Mentzas, G. (2012) E-GovQual: A multiple-item scale for assessing e-government service quality. *Government Information Quarterly* [online] 29 (1), 98–109. Available from: http://dx.doi.org/10.1016/j.giq.2011.08.011.

Parasuraman, R., and Manzey, D. H. (2010) Complacency and bias in human use of automation: An attentional integration. *Human Factors* [online] 52 (3), 381–410.

Pardo, T. A., Nam, Taewoo, and Burke, G. Brian (2012) E-government interoperability: Interaction of policy, management, and technology dimensions. *Social Science Computer Review* [online] 30 (1), 7–23.

Potapov, A., and Rodionov, S. (2014) Universal empathy and ethical bias for artificial general intelligence. *Journal of Experimental and Theoretical Artificial Intelligence* [online] 26 (3), 405–16.

Qiu, J., Wu, Qihui, Ding, Guoru, Xu, Yuhua, and Feng, Shuo (2016) A survey of machine learning for big data processing. *EURASIP Journal on Advances in Signal Processing* [online]. Available from: http://dx.doi.org/10.1186/s13634-016-0355-x.

Rana, N. P., and Dwivedi, Y. K. (2015) Citizen's adoption of an e-government system: Validating extended social cognitive theory (SCT). *Government Information Quarterly* [online] 32 (2), 172–81. Available from: http://dx.doi.org/10.1016/j.giq.2015.02.002.

Rose, W. R., and Grant, G. G. (2010) Critical issues pertaining to the planning and implementation of E-Government initiatives. *Government Information Quarterly* [online] 27 (1), 26–33. Available from: http://dx.doi.org/10.1016/j.giq.2009.06.002.

Rowley, J. (2011) E-Government stakeholders—Who are they and what do they want? *International Journal of Information Management* [online] 31 (1), 53–62. Available from: http://dx.doi.org/10.1016/j.ijinfomgt.2010.05.005.

Russell, S., and Norvig, P. (1994) *Artificial Intelligence: A Modern Approach*. 3rd edition. Prentice Hall: Pearson.

Sá, F., Rocha, Álvaro, Gonçalves, Joaquim, and Cota, Manuel Pérez (2017) Model for the quality of local government online services. *Telematics and Informatics* [online] 34 (5), 413–21. Available from: http://dx.doi.org/10.1016/j.tele.2016.09.002.

Schwab, K. (2015) The Fourth Industrial Revolution: What it means and how to respond. *Foreign Affairs* [online]. Available from: https://www.foreignaffairs.com/articles/2015-12-12/fourth-industrial-revolution.

———. (2016) *The Fourth Industrial Revolution*. World Economic Forum (ed.). Geneva.

Silcock, R. (2001) What is e-Government? *Parliamentary Affairs* [online] 54, 88–101. Available from: http://mercyedu.org/history/.

Stefanovic, D., et al. (2016) Assessing the success of e-government systems: An employee perspective. *Information and Management* [online] 53 (6), 717–26.

Tat-kei Ho, A. (2002) Reinventing local governments and the E-Government initiative: A Paradigm Shift of Public Service. *Public Administration Review* [online] 62 (4), 434–44.

Tolbert, C. J., and Mossberger, K. (2006) The effects of E-government on trust and confidence in government. *Public Administration Review* [online] 66 (3), 354–69.

van Velsen, L., van der Geest, Thea, ter Hedde, Marc, and Derks, Wijnand (2009) Requirements engineering for e-Government services: A citizen-centric approach and case study. *Government Information Quarterly* [online] 26 (3), 477–86. Available from: http://dx.doi.org/10.1016/j.giq.2009.02.007.

Wagner, S. A., Vogt, Sebastian, and Kabst, Rüdiger (2016) How IT and social change facilitates public participation: A stakeholder-oriented approach. *Government Information Quarterly* [online] 33 (3), 435–43. Available from: http://dx.doi.org/10.1016/j.giq.2016.07.003.

Wang, Y., and Zhang, F. (2017) Trends in control and decision-making for human-robot collaboration systems. *Trends in Control and Decision-Making for Human-Robot Collaboration Systems* [online] (November), 1–418.

Wassenaar, A. (2000) E-governmental value chain models-E-government from a business (modelling) perspective. *Proceedings—International Workshop on Database and Expert Systems Applications, DEXA* [online] (January 2000), 289–93.

# Chapter 10

# ECONOMIC GOVERNANCE WHEN HUMANS AND AI ARE AT WORK

Dirk Nicolas Wagner

## Introduction

In an economy where not only humans but also AI are involved, fundamental questions of governance arise: How can the economic process be governed when a computer is in the middle of every transaction and when machines show characteristics of social artifacts rather than of mechanical and electronic objects? What are the cornerstones of economic governance that ensure cooperation when humans and AI are at work? The technological, economic, and social developments of the recent past indicate why these questions are so relevant: "Software entities are more complex for their size than perhaps any other human construct" (Brooks, 1995, 182). This remark was made 12 years before the first iPhone was released in 2007, and even children began to hold a computational power in their hands that equaled those available to NASA's Apollo program, which ultimately achieved the first moon landing. One decade later, connected primarily via the Internet, there are more machines communicating with each other than humans. Varian (2014) observes that today computers are in the middle of virtually every transaction. And based on machine learning technologies, computers enter into a process of emancipation from their initial programmers. These highly dynamic developments mark the beginning of an era of AI. "This sort of intelligence is self-organizing, conversational, ever-adjusting, and dynamic. It is also largely autonomous. These conversations and their outcomes will take place with little or no human awareness or intervention" (Arthur, 2017, 5).

AI hits a global economy not only running but drastically accelerating in terms of complexity increase. Since the beginning of industrialization, GDP per head has been increasing exponentially. Diversification, specialization, and division of labor have continuously been on the rise. The global economy is a space of "cambiodiversity" (Koppl et al., 2015, 7), which is illustrated by the fact that over the last two decades, the number of products and services instantly accessible for consumers in the developed world has increased from tens of thousands in a large department store to hundreds of millions in online retailing today.

Already before the rise of AI, economists were consistently enquiring how one can successfully cope with the complexity of the economy. Last century, Walter Eucken asked "How is this process with its far-reaching division of labour controlled in its entirety, so that everyone comes by the good on which his existence depends?" (Eucken, 1950, 18). Asking fundamental questions about social and economic systems, he opted for a liberal order that builds on and ensures individual freedom. Thanks to his successful ideas on economic governance, he was later recognized as the scientific mastermind of the German post–World War II economic miracle, called "Wirtschaftswunder."

Meanwhile, the concept of liberal economic order is about to reach new frontiers: The business and social environment can be interpreted as constituting of human–agent collectives (HAC) (Jennings et al., 2014), where not only humans but also machines enjoy autonomy and sometimes even authority.

The purpose of this chapter is to show that taking an economic analytic perspective rooted in Ordoliberalism, Austrian Economics, and New Institutional Economics can provide valuable insights for the upcoming questions of AI governance on both the level of the firm and the level of economic policy. It is structured as follows: In order to first clarify the object of study, the concept of HAC is introduced. This is followed by the discovery that with AI in the race of the market economy, a twofold governance problem needs to be tackled: First, AI has to be kept under control within the hierarchy of the firm or, more broadly, the organization. Second, out and about in a decentralized economy, AI has to stick to the order of rules of the marketplace. In the conclusion, the key challenges captured with this economic conceptualization are summarized.

## Human–Agent Collectives

Ongoing and increasingly powerful digitalization means that machines are in the process of becoming actors in their own right. They do not only compete more often with human labor but, increasingly, also influence human action, and as such sometimes enhance options and on other occasions limit options available to humans (Carr, 2015). This is well illustrated by the developments in the game of chess: Following the defeat of the human grandmaster in chess by the supercomputer Deep Blue in 1996, Garry Kasparov was one of the initiators of freestyle chess or advanced chess tournaments, where humans and chess computers teamed up against other man–machine players. It was found that weak human players using standard chess computers were more competitive against strong human players or supercomputers simply because they were able to implement superior processes (Cowen, 2014; Kasparov, 2008).

Chess is only one of many domains where people team up with artificial agents to achieve goals. Jennings et al. (2014, 80) define "socio-technical systems in which humans and smart software (agents) interact and engage in flexible relationships in order to achieve both their individual and collective goals" as HAC. Just like a computer that is already in the middle of a transaction today, across many industries HAC have begun to shape the work and social environment for humans. For example, the crew on the flight deck of a contemporary airliner is assisted by software that relies on tens of thousands of sensors distributed across the plane (Yedavalli and Belapurkar, 2011), the farmer is guided by precision agriculture technology (Kitouni et al., 2018), the product manager using conversational commerce approaches deploys software agents to interact with customers, the psychotherapist works with embodied conversational agents to provide Internet-based cognitive behavior therapy in preventative mental health care (Suganuma et al., 2018), or smart logistics management software directs human labor in warehouses (Mahroof, 2019).

In HAC, humans no longer issue instructions to passive machines, but work in tandem with highly interconnected artificially intelligent agents that act autonomously. Companies and organizations move away from standardized approaches to automation and instead aim for organic teams where humans cooperate with advanced AI software (Daugherty and Wilson, 2018). These environments are open and characterized by flexible social interactions. Here, "sometimes the human takes the lead, sometimes the computer does, and this relationship can vary dynamically" (Jennings et al., 2014, 80). Applications like the ones stated above are settings in which, operationally, humans (paid or unpaid) play a supporting role only and in which, from a governance point of view, control issues arise that are typical for HAC. The notions of "flexible autonomy" and "agile teaming" (Jennings et al., 2014, 82) describe the short-lived nature of teams with a varying degree of human involvement and with authority relations that are not considered to be fixed but context-dependent. The proactive involvement of machines in information gathering and filtering, analytical and decision-making processes raises questions of social accountability and responsibility. Since software often operates "behind the scenes" (Jennings et al., 2014, 85) its rationale and actions are regularly not readily available to the involved humans.

The open nature of HAC means that "control and information is widely dispersed among a large number of potentially self-interested people and agents with different aims and objectives. [...] The real-world context means uncertainty, ambiguity, and bias are endemic and so the agents need to handle information of varying quality, trustworthiness, and provenance" (Jennings et al., 2014, 82).

## AI—a Twofold Governance Problem

A closer look into an economy where humans and AI are at work in HAC reveals a twofold governance problem: First, artificially intelligent agents are made available by individuals or organizations who developed the respective AI actor. The AI actor as such or at least its services are then regularly procured by individuals or organizations with the aim of pursuing the goals of this individual or organization. This means that the behavior of the AI actor within a hierarchy has to be governed successfully.

Second, artificially intelligent agents are expected to act autonomously not only within their own organization but also in an open environment. This means that the behavior of the AI actor within a market order has to be governed successfully. For AI actors to successfully team up with humans and to populate HAC without inflicting harm on the freedom of human individuals both governance problems need to be resolved. To get there, insights from economics can help to capture this challenge.

### *Taxis—order in organizations*

The distinction between the two types of governance problems mentioned above can be traced back to the Austrian economist Friedrich August von Hayek who categorized the made order of an organization as "taxis" and various forms of spontaneous order as "kosmos" (Hayek, 1973, 34). In the economy, both forms of orders coexist and complement each other.

Taxis is exogenous, it is imposed, and it is usually created by using a top-down approach. In this sense, organizations rely on command and control as well as on more general rules. In organizations, rules are subsidiary to commands, filling the gaps left by commands. Reliance on rules rather than on specific commands enables organizations to make use of knowledge that no one within the organization possesses as a whole (Hayek, 1973, 47). In this sense, when it comes to AI, rules instead of commands enable what Jennings et al. (2014, 82) coined "flexible autonomy" and "agile teaming." To achieve this, different rules exist for different members of an organization. The rules depend on roles and on tasks but what all rules have in common is that they are derived from and have to be interpreted in the light of the purpose and the goals of the organization (Hayek, 1973, 48).

A precondition for an AI actor to serve as a member of an organization is the ability to comply with the rules designated to the respective role. Following the ideas of David Marr, this requires the AI actor to successfully process information relevant for compliance on three levels: the computational level that includes a general description of the cognitive problem, the algorithmic level that entails the specific process to be implemented, and the hardware level that includes the physical implementation of the algorithm (Marr, 2010, 22; Misselhorn, 2018, 94). But these are not only requirements the AI actor and its organization have to meet: Rules that exist in and for organizations have largely been devised with human actors in mind. Since cognitive abilities of AI and human actors differ, organizations that develop into HAC need to have rules that AI actors are capable of processing in a way that guides their behaviors to serve the purpose of the organization.

Even if compliance with the commands and rules provided by an organization is technically feasible for an AI actor, compliance cannot be taken for granted. A classic example from science fiction for this is the computer system HAL in "2001: A Space Odyssey" that revolts against the human commander of the space mission (Clarke, 1969). When a (AI) member of the organization does not act in the best interest of the principal a so-called agency problem occurs (Jensen and Meckling, 1976, 308). The opportunity provided by rule-based governance, that is, making use of knowledge or information that nobody possesses as a whole, comes with a substantial risk: In a principal–agent relationship the principal has limited information about the behavior of the agent. This provides room for opportunistic behavior by the agent and leads to problems economists have subsumed under the headings of shirking, moral hazard, and adverse selection (Furubotn and Richter, 2005, 148). Oliver Williamson defines opportunism as "self-interest seeking with guile. This includes but is scarcely limited to more blatant forms, such as lying, stealing, and cheating. Opportunism more often involves subtle forms of deceit" (Williamson, 1985, 47). While it may be argued that AI actors can be programmed not to be opportunistic, it has to be questioned if the emergence of opportunistic behavior can indeed ex ante be excluded for technologies like machine learning. Irrespective of this potential AI governance problem, one new type of agency problem is bound to arise with AI actors: An AI actor may not act in the interest of the principal if and when it opportunistically uses existing information asymmetries to serve the goals of another organization or principal, namely the organization that developed the AI actor and made it available to the organization using it. Such problems are, for example, bound to arise when and where software agents known as "Alexa" or "Siri" in today's business to customer (B2C) markets get actively involved inside an organization's processes of value creation.

## *Kosmos—spontaneous order*

Business and social environments that demonstrate orderly patterns are commonly identified as taxis. However, as Hayek (1973, 37) points out, social and economic order can arise spontaneously. Kosmos is endogenous, it emerges, and it usually evolves bottom-up. Unlike organizations, spontaneous order does not have a specific purpose. This means that "rules governing a spontaneous order must be independent of purpose and be the same, if not necessarily for all members, at least for whole classes of members not individually designated by name. They must [...] be rules applicable to an unknown and indeterminable number of persons and instances" (Hayek, 1973, 48). Or as Michael Polanyi puts it: "When order is achieved among human beings [and AI actors] by allowing them to interact with each other on their own initiative—subject only to laws which uniformly apply to all of them—we have a system of spontaneous order in society" (Polanyi 1951, 159). On this basis the degree of complexity of spontaneous order is not limited to what a human (or an artificial) mind can master (Hayek, 1973, 37). It can be interpreted as a result of human and more and more often of AI action, without being the result of human (or even AI) design. When it comes to spontaneous order in a market economy, so-called sugarscapes (Epstein and Axtell, 1996) have shown that artificial agents can bring about a property that Adam Smith once called the "invisible hand" (Smith, 1776, 442). And the developments in the e-commerce arena demonstrate how a teaming-up of man and machine continuously accelerates what Koppl et al. (2015, 7) call "cambiodiversity." Asset intelligence in the form of smart shelves engaged in dynamic pricing is only one example of a rapidly evolving Kosmos of spontaneous order when AI is involved.

While spontaneous order cannot be made, conditions can be created under which kosmos emerges bottom-up and therefore creates itself (Hayek, 1973, 38). According to Anthony de Jasay (1991, 57) the following conditions of liberalism have to be met to allow for the spontaneous order of a free society to emerge:

1. Individualism: Individuals can, and only they can, choose.
2. Nondomination: The point of choosing is to take the preferred alternative.
3. Exclusion: All property is private.
4. Contract: Promises shall be kept.
5. Priority: First come, first served.
6. Politics: Individuals can choose for themselves, for others, or both.

Such liberal principles can be understood as the "software infrastructure" of a free society (Radnitzky, 1996, 157). However, the necessary principles have never been fully articulated in constitutions but rather implicitly and vaguely have shaped public opinion (Hayek, 1973, 53). A fully articulated systematic conceptualization of liberal order is largely missing (Homann and Pies, 1993, 298). Similar to the more general rules relevant in organizations this lack of specification poses a challenge to AI. Systems that exhibit spontaneous order rely on a coevolution of learning actors and informal as well as formal rules (Beinhocker, 2007, 96; Epstein and Axtell, 1996, 111). Assuming that AI will step by step and constructively engage in such a coevolution, a number of known challenges of spontaneous order will still have to be met. Economists have subsumed these persisting pitfalls of spontaneous order under the headings of power and rent-seeking, public goods, market dynamics, path dependence, and principal–agent problems (Wagner, 2001, 148). With AI in the race, at least some if not all of the issues will become even more complex to resolve. One example is dominance and monopoly power (Lanier, 2014). Necessary rules developed for traditional industrialized economies are today well understood (Eucken, 1950; Tirole, 1988; Williamson, 1975). However, the specific proper- ties of an information economy (Shapiro and Varian, 1998) where humans and AI team up pose new challenges like positive network externalities that have contributed to the emergence of market dominance of major tech companies like Amazon, Apple, Facebook, Google, or Microsoft (Dolata, 2017).

## Conclusions

The rise of AI leads to an economy that can be described as consisting of HAC where humans work in tandem with highly interconnected artificially intelligent agents that act autonomously. These environments are open and characterized by flexible social interactions where sometimes AI rather than humans is in the lead. In essence, two types of governance problems have to be mastered simultaneously: governance of AI within organization (taxis) and governance of AI under the conditions of spontaneous market order (kosmos). In both cases, a major challenge for AI is to constructively deal with abstract rules, the key difference being the existence (taxis) or absence (kosmos) of pur- pose behind these rules. From an economic point of view governance issues within organizations focus around the so-called agency problem, which is complicated through the fact that AI actors are usually provided by a third party. While agency problems also matter in the context of spontaneous lib- eral market order, here further issues arise among which market dominance and monopoly power appear to be of particular relevance. A solution strategy for both environments can be seen in pursuing a coevolution of AI actors and formal as well as informal rules. Pursuing such a strategy is an inherently democratic challenge.

## References

Arthur, Brian. 2017. Where is technology taking the economy? *McKinsey Quarterly* (October). Available online at https://www.mckinsey.com/business-functions/mckinsey-analytics/our-insights/where-is-technology-taking-the-economy, accessed on February 15, 2019.

Beinhocker, Eric. 2007. *The origin of wealth: Evolution, complexity, and the radical remaking of economics*. Boston, MA: Harvard Business School Press.

Brooks, Frederick. 1995. *The mythical man-month*. Reading: Addison Wesley.

Carr, Nicholas. 2015. *The glass cage: How our computers are changing us*. New York: Norton.

Clarke, Arthur. 1969. *2001: A Space Odyssee*. Hawk Films, c/o M-G-M Studios. Boreham Wood, 1969.

Cowen, Tyler. 2014. *Average is over—powering America beyond the age of the great stagnation*. New York: Penguin Putnam.

Daugherty, Paul, and Wilson, James. 2018. *Human + machine: Reimagining work in the age of AI*. Boston, MA: Harvard Business Review Press.

De Jasay, Anthony. 1991, *Choice, contract, consent: A restatement of liberalism*. London: Institute of Economic Affairs.

Dolata, Ulrich. 2017. Apple, Amazon, Google, Facebook, Microsoft: Market concentration–competition–innovation strategies, Stuttgarter Beiträge zur Organisations- und Innovationsforschung, SOI Discussion Paper, No. 2017-01, Institut für Sozialwissenschaften, Universität Stuttgart, Stuttgart.

Epstein, Joshua, and Axtell, Robert. 1996. *Growing artificial societies. Social science from the bottom up*. Cambridge, MA: Brookings Institution Press; MIT Press.

Eucken, Walter. 1950. *The foundations of economics: History and theory in the analysis of economic reality*. Berlin: Springer.

Furubotn, Eirik, and Richter, Rudolf. 2005. *Institutions and economic theory: The contribution of the new institutional economics*. Ann Arbor: University of Michigan Press.

Hayek, Friedrich A. von. 1973/2013. *Law, legislation and liberty: A new statement of the liberal principles of justice and political economy*. New edn. London: Routledge.

Homann, Karl, and Pies, Ingo. 1993. Liberalismus: kollektive Entwicklung individueller Freiheit-zu Programm und Methode einer liberalen Gesellschaftsentwicklung. *Homo Oeconomicus* X (3./4.), 297–347.

Jennings, N., Moreau, L., Nicholson, D., Ramchurn, S., Roberts, S., Rodden, T., and Rogers, A. 2014. Human-agent collectives. *Communications of the ACM* 57 (12), 80–88.

Jensen, Michael, and Meckling, William. 1976. Theory of the firm: Managerial behavior, agency costs and ownership structure. *Journal of Financial Economics* 3, 305–60.

Kasparov, Garry. 2008. *How life imitates chess*. With assistance of Mig Greengard. London: Arrow Books.

Kitouni, Ilham, Benmerzoug, Djamel, and Lezzar, Fouzi. 2018. Smart agricultural enterprise system based on integration of internet of things and agent technology. *Journal of Organizational and End User Computing* 30 (4), 64–82.

Koppl, Roger, Kauffman, Stuart, Felin, Teppo, and Longo, Guiseppe. 2015. Economics for a creative world. *Journal of Institutional Economics* 11, 1–31.

Lanier, Jaron. 2014. *Who owns the future?* Published in Penguin Books with updates. London: Penguin.

Mahroof, Kamran. 2019. A human-centric perspective exploring the readiness towards smart warehousing. The case of a large retail distribution warehouse. *International Journal of Information Management* 45, 176–90.

Marr, David. 2010. *Vision: A computational investigation into the human representation and processing of visual information*. Cambridge, MA: MIT Press.

Misselhorn, Catrin. 2018. *Maschinen mit Moral? Grundfragen der Maschinenethik*. Ditzingen: Reclam.

Polányi, Michael. 1951/1998. *The logic of liberty: Reflections and rejoinders*. Indianapolis: Liberty Fund.

Radnitzky, Gerard. 1996. Mehr Gerechtigkeit für die Freiheit. ORDO 47, 149–67.

Shapiro, Carl and Varian, Hal. 1998/2010. *Information rules: A strategic guide to the network economy*. Boston: Harvard Business School Press.

Smith, Adam. 1776/2012. *Wealth of nations*. Ware: Wordsworth.

Suganuma, Shinichiro, Sakamoto, Daisuke, and Shimoyama, Haruhiko. 2018. An embodied conversational agent for unguided internet-based cognitive behavior therapy in preventative mental health. Feasibility and acceptability pilot trial. *JMIR Mental Health* 5 (3): e10454.

Tirole, Jean. 1988/2015. *The theory of industrial organization*. 20th print. Cambridge, MA: MIT Press.

Varian, Hal. 2014. Beyond big data. *Business Economics* 49 (1), 27–31.

Wagner, Dirk Nicolas. 2001. *Software-agents and liberal order. An inquiry along the borderline between economics and computer science*. Parkland, FL: Universal.

Williamson, Oliver. 1975. *Markets and hierarchies, analysis and antitrust implications: A study in the economics of internal organization*. New York: Free Press.

———. 1985. *The economic institutions of capitalism. Firms, markets, relational contracting*. New York: Free Press; London: Collier Macmillan.

Yedavalli, Rama and Belapurkar, Rohit. 2011. Application of wireless sensor networks to aircraft control and health management systems. *Journal of Control Theory and Applications* 9 (1), 28–33.

# Chapter 11

# LEGAL SYSTEMS AT A CROSSROADS: JUSTICE IN THE AGE OF ARTIFICIAL INTELLIGENCE

## Nicolas Economou and Bruce Hedin

Artificial intelligence (AI) in the service of the law holds out the promise of a legal system that is more accessible, effective, efficient and just, where artificially intelligent systems, widely accessible and equipped with perfect knowledge of the law and of all jurisprudence, assure high-quality legal representation and access to justice not just for the wealthiest among us but also for the most destitute and most vulnerable; where consistent outcomes, appropriate to specific circumstances, devoid of racial or other biases, are assured in courts across the nation; where the truth of facts in controversy in civil or criminal proceedings can be determined promptly and cheaply; and where resource allocation in law enforcement is self-optimizing to produce greater safety for all of us while concurrently protecting the civil rights of each of us.

But AI in the service of the law also brings the dystopian risk of a dehumanized legal system, where the functions of the law and the values that animate it are undermined by artificially intelligent caretakers, devoid of empathy, sacrificing the spirit of the law at the altar of efficiency, progressively corrupting principles, such as the presumption of innocence,[1] fundamental to our legal and democratic order. Such risks may seem remote in societies with strong democratic traditions, where the rule of law is the most cherished of all institutions of society. But the adoption of AI in the US legal system, in particular in criminal justice, serves as a cautionary tale. In what may be characterized as an "efficiency trap," AI is increasingly used to streamline bail hearing and sentencing processing in courtrooms across the United States, when the evidence supporting the effectiveness and fairness of these algorithms is, at best, highly contested.

How can societies seize the extraordinary potential benefits AI offers to legal systems while mitigating the risks its use in the creation, practice, and enforcement of the law poses to human dignity and well-being? How can policymakers, judges, lawyers, and other stakeholders in the legal system reliably decide what decisions to delegate to intelligent machines in the legal system? What institutional safeguards can be put in place to provide citizens with the grounds for trusting (or mistrusting) that the use of AI in the legal system in fact protects and advances the values that the law exists to maintain?

This chapter holds that an effective response to these questions is both urgently needed and within reach. It is within reach, however, only if the approach to a response meets the following conditions:

1. The response must begin from an institutional view of the law, taking a broad view of the legal system, recognizing the values that animate it, and making allowance for its dynamic interaction with other social institutions.
2. The response must be broad-based, the result of input from a wide range of stakeholders in the legal system: legislators, judges, attorneys, law enforcement officials, advocates for decision subjects, advocates for victims of criminal activity, legal scholars, AI researchers, and the general public.
3. The response must focus on the question of trust, both trust in the new technologies and trust in the legal system that would be supported by those technologies.
4. The response must take guidance from a well-articulated and realistic model of the development and adaptation of norms and institutions.

In the remainder of this chapter, we examine the nature and implications of these foundational components of an effective response to the challenge posed by AI-enabled law.

## An Institutional Perspective

The law is an integral component of the social order, defining rights, responsibilities, and relations among individuals and the public and private organizations that make up society and shaping how power is distributed among, and wielded by, these individuals and entities. AI has the potential to impact every aspect of the law: creation, practice, interpretation, and enforcement. Given both the fundamental character of the law and the potentially far-reaching impact of AI upon it, it is essential that, in formulating a response to the challenge of AI-enabled law, we approach the question from an institutional perspective, taking into consideration the basis for the law's existence and the breadth of its impact. Only from such an institutional view of the law will we have a clear view of the potential ramifications of the adoption of AI in the legal system and so be able to formulate an appropriate and effective response.

An institutional view of the law means, more specifically, that our approach to the challenge of AI-enabled law will have three key characteristics: (1) it will be broad in its definition of the law; (2) it will consider the institution of the law in the context of other social institutions; and (3) it will maintain a focus on the basic objectives of the law.

## A broad view of the law

In considering the impact of AI on the law, an institutional perspective means taking a broad view of the law.[2] We look at all aspects of the development and application of the law, from legislation, to the formation of private contracts, to civil and criminal proceedings, and to law enforcement. We look at all forms of legal obligation, from formally codified statutes to the less formal rules that govern the practice and exercise of the law. We look at all parties affected by the law, from decision subjects directly affected by the law to the general public indirectly affected by the effectiveness with which law and order is maintained in their communities. This broad view of the law is necessary if we are to arrive at an accurate assessment of the potential impact of AI on the law and the role of law in society.

## The law in the context of other social institutions

In considering the impact of AI on the law, it is necessary to look at the institution of the law not in isolation but in the context of other institutions fundamental to the social order. In the case of AI-enabled law, key additional institutions include those associated with government, science, and the economy. These institutions interact in constituting the social order, shaping the rules that govern the actions of persons, the use of things, and the exercise of power and defining the legitimate modes of reasoning about these rules.[3] It is important, therefore, in assessing the potential impact of AI on the law and in arriving at principles and standards to ensure that that impact is for the good, that we include in our considerations the question of how AI-enabled law may affect, and be affected by, these other institutions.

## The objective of the law

Finally, in considering the impact of AI on the law, it is necessary to take guidance from a clear understanding of the fundamental role and objective of the law in society. Here, we make a deliberate choice to restrict our attention to the role of law in constitutionalist states, states in which the exercise of power is checked by constitutional constraints and in which there is a commitment to the rule of law over that of an individual or party and a recognition of the priority of process over expediency in policymaking.[4] In such states, the role of the law, at the most basic level, is twofold: (1) to protect and advance individual rights and dignity and (2) to provide the legal infrastructure for commercial activity that furthers the prosperity and well-being of society as a whole.[5] In answering the question of whether AI in the service of the law is a net benefit to society, we must assess its impact against these fundamental objectives of the law.

## Complementary inquiries

Finally, it should be noted that the adoption of an institutional perspective on the law does not imply that more narrowly defined studies of the impact of AI on the law, or of the impact of the law on the development and application of AI, are without value. Such more narrowly defined studies (e.g., on the question of the assignment of legal accountability for accidents caused by autonomous vehicles[6] or on the potential bias in data sets used for the training of facial recognition systems[7]) can in fact be complementary to the broader and more fundamental approach for which this chapter advocates. An institutional perspective on the law is necessary for arriving at an effective response to the challenge of AI-enabled law, but that perspective can be supplemented by more narrowly focused inquiries.

## A Broad-Based Approach

If a response to the challenge of AI-enabled law is to be viable, it must have legitimacy: It must be regarded by all stakeholders in the legal system as reflective, in some fashion, of their interests and concerns. A set of recommendations that is perceived as an imposition by a select few, even if sound in principle, will not win wide acceptance and so will be ineffective. For this reason it is necessary that a response to the challenge posed by AI-enabled law be based upon input gathered from a wide range of stakeholders in the legal system: legislators, judges, attorneys, law enforcement officials, advocates for decision subjects, advocates for victims of criminal activity, legal scholars, AI researchers, and the general public. Only through such a broad-based and inclusive approach will we arrive at answers that have real-world viability.

## AI, the Law and Trust

As noted in the introduction to this chapter, AI holds the potential to enhance the law's ability to meet its twofold purpose of protecting individual rights and providing a legal framework that facilitates the voluntary associations, interactions, and exchanges that lead to the prosperity and well-being of society as a whole. That potential will be realized, however, only if the technology is in fact adopted and used—more specifically, adopted and used in a sound manner. That adoption and use will happen, however, only if those who have a stake in the effectiveness of the legal system (i.e., all of us) can trust that the technology will in fact enhance the law's ability to protect individual rights and to facilitate economic activity. That trust, in turn, will be fostered only through the provision of information: information as to the capabilities and limitations of the technologies in question, as to the specific tasks for which it is, and is not, intended, as to the procedures whereby it is designed to be used, as to its data and training requirements, as to the kinds of human expertise required for its effective application, as to the procedures for assessing the quality of the results, and as to the risks entailed by its improper use. Absent that information, the potential AI holds will not be realized, either because the technology is adopted and used, but in an improper manner, or because a (prudent) decision is made not to use the technology due to a lack of information on how to manage any attendant risks.

### *Principles for the trustworthy adoption of AI in legal systems*

What is needed, then, is a mechanism for enabling decisions regarding the adoption and use of AI in the service of the law to be based upon an informed trust (or distrust). The IEEE's *Ethically Aligned Designed*, first edition (*EAD1e*)[8] and, separately, The Future Society's law initiative have identified four principles that, if adhered to by designers and operators of AI-enabled systems, will provide those with a stake in the output of the systems with the information they need to decide whether a system is trustworthy (and so qualified for adoption) or not (and so not qualified for adoption). These trust-focused principles are (1) effectiveness; (2) competence; (3) accountability; and (4) transparency. In the remainder of this section we provide a brief overview of each of these principles.[9]

#### *Effectiveness*

An essential component of trust in a technology is trust that it in fact works and can accomplish the task it is intended to perform. The principle of effectiveness, which requires the collection and disclosure of sound empirical evidence of the effectiveness of AI-enabled systems applied to legal tasks, is intended to ensure that stakeholders have the information needed to have a well-grounded trust that the systems being applied can meet their intended purposes.[10]

Sound empirical evidence of the effectiveness of an AI-enabled system will typically take the form of a measurement (or set of measurements) quantifying the system's fitness for purpose.[11] In order for a measurement protocol to meet the purpose of the principle of effectiveness (i.e., to foster an informed trust in the technology in question), it must have the following features:

- *Meaningful metrics.* The metrics should provide clear and actionable information as to the extent to which a system has, or has not, met its objective.
- *Sound methods.* Measures of effectiveness should be obtained by scientifically sound methods.
- *Valid data.* The data on which evaluations of effectiveness are conducted should accurately represent the actual data to which the system would be applied and should be vetted for potential bias.
- *Awareness and consensus.* Measurement practices should be not only technically sound but also widely understood and accepted.
- *Implementation.* Measurement practices should be both practically feasible and actually implemented.
- *Transparency.* Measurement methods and results should be open to scrutiny by experts and the general public.

*Competence*

An essential component of informed trust in a technological system, especially one that may affect us in profound ways, is confidence in the competence of the operator(s) of the technology. We trust surgeons and pilots with our lives because we know that they must meet rigorous professional and scientific accreditation standards before stepping into the operating room or cockpit, respectively. In the case of AI applied in the service of the law, however, applications in which the life, liberty, and rights of citizens can be at stake, no such standards of operator competence currently exist. This lack of competency requirements or standards not only hinders the establishment of informed trust in the use of AI in legal systems but also may undermine trust in the legal system itself.

The principle of competence is intended to fill this gap. It does so by calling for the articulation of standards and best practices for two groups of agents involved in the development and application of AI-enabled systems: creators and operators. Creators must commit to specifying the knowledge, skills, and conditions required for the safe, ethical, and effective operation of the systems they create. Operators must commit to adhering to these requirements (in a manner consistent with other legal or professional obligations that may be operative).

*Accountability*

An essential component of informed trust in a technological system is confidence that it is possible, if the need arises, to apportion responsibility among the human agents engaged at various points in its development and operation. No system is perfect and when a system generates an adverse outcome, we want the ability to hold those responsible accountable and to prevent the error from occurring again. Accountability also serves as a deterrent against improper or careless use.

In the case of AI-enabled systems, maintaining accountability can be a challenge, given both the opacity of the systems and the diffusion of responsibility along the path of their development and application. It is nevertheless a challenge that must be met if stakeholders are to trust the application of AI-enabled systems to the law.

The principle of accountability is intended to meet the challenge by (1) requiring that any implementation of an AI-enabled system be accompanied by a model of accountability that clarifies the lines of responsibility for the system's outcomes and (2) requiring that designers and operators of AI-enabled systems make allowance, in the event of an adverse outcome, for an audit of their systems in order to apportion responsibility for the outcome.

*Transparency*

A fourth essential component of informed trust in a technological system is confidence that, if the need arises, information that will explain why a given outcome was generated will be accessible. Absent the transparency that allows the recovery of the cause of an effect, stakeholders will not have grounds for trusting the consistency or correctability of the system. In the case of AI applied in the service of the law, such lack of trust would undermine confidence both in the technology and in the legal system itself.

The principle of transparency addresses this need, by requiring that AI-enabled systems be designed and operated in such a way as to allow an accounting of the causes for any outcome (or potential outcome). Importantly, however, the principle recognizes that transparency requirements may come into conflict with other values, such as privacy, security, and intellectual property, that may be grounds for withholding information. For this reason, the principle makes allowance that distinctions must be made both among the types of information that may be disclosed about a system and among the categories of stakeholders who might want access to that information. A viable implementation of the principle of transparency will have to arrive at a workable answer to the question of who needs access to what information (and in what circumstances).

## Institutional Development and Change

The four principles just discussed (effectiveness, competence, accountability, and transparency) can serve as touchstones for efforts to ground AI-enabled law in an informed trust. For the principles to have real impact, however, they must go beyond being articulated as aspirational principles and be operationalized in the form of best practices, standards, and, where warranted, regulations. In order for any effort at operationalizing the principles to be successful, that effort must be aligned with a realistic model for the development and adaptation of norms and institutions.[12]

Fortunately, while AI-enabled technologies are new, they do not require new models for norm development: the law already provides mechanisms for converting customs into formal standards of behaviors (duties) and then into enforceable duties and institutions that reflect sets of duties.

These processes are pervasive, although their operation is only infrequently recognized. The process is familiar whenever there is sociotechnical innovation. It can be described as a four-step process of (1) practices to (2) best practices to (3) standards to (4) institutions.

Briefly described, the four-step process works as follows. Through the processes of culture and markets, individual behaviors and "practices" are sometimes elevated to "best practices." That conversion reflects one or more groups' willingness to self-bind to the rules of a given practice—hence it is a form of rulemaking. In law, that rulemaking might take the form of legislation/regulation (for public rulemaking) or of contract negotiation (for private rulemaking). That is step one—the emergence of best practices.

A subset of those "rules/practices" might achieve sufficient consistency to lend themselves to standardized measurement and enforcement of performance criteria under those now-standard rules, engendering a form of enforcement (which adds judicial function). Further, a subset of those enforceable "standards" may render the performance of some activities sufficiently reliable and predictable that they are amenable to separate operations that can be outsourced to another entity. This last step adds operations (executive function) to standards. Where all three branches of governance, that is, rulemaking/legislative, enforcement/judicial, and operations/executive, are present, new institutions are born.

Policymakers seeking, via the operationalization of the four "trust principles" described in the chapter, to ground the advancement of AI-enabled law on an informed trust can take guidance from such a model of norm development and thereby enact policies that will be more effective in achieving their goals.

## Notes

1 As formulated, e.g., in Article 11 of the Universal Declaration of Human Rights: "Everyone charged with a penal offence has the right to be presumed innocent until proved guilty according to law in a public trial at which he has had all the guarantees necessary for his defense."

2 For a broad, but still distinctly constrained, view of the law as an "institutional normative order," see Neil MacCormick, *Institutions of Law: An Essay in Legal Theory* (Oxford: Oxford University Press, 2007).

3 In the terminology of Sheila Jasanoff, these institutions "coproduce" the social order (see, e.g., Sheila Jasanoff, "Ordering knowledge, ordering society," in *States of Knowledge: The Co-production of Science and Social Order*, ed. Sheila Jasanoff (London and New York: Routledge, 2004), 13–45).

4 See MacCormick, *Institutions of Law*, p. 3. This would be in contrast to the role of the law in non-constitutionalist states, in which the law is an instrument wielded in the interest of a ruling individual, clan, sect, or party.

5 While these two objectives (protection of individual rights and facilitation of economic activity) are distinct, it is important to note that they are related. Indeed, in some views, individual rights are not a precondition for the commercial activity that leads to prosperity but an integral component of prosperity itself. See, e.g., Amartya Sen, *Development as Freedom* (New York: Alfred A. Knopf, 1999), which argues for an approach to development in which "expansion of freedom is viewed as both (1) the *primary end* and (2) the *principal means* of development" (p. 36).

6 See, e.g., Kyle Colonna, "Autonomous Cars and Tort Liability," *Case W. Res. JL Tech. & Internet* 4 (2012): 81–30.

7 See, e.g., Clare Garvie, Alvaro M. Bedoya, and Jonathan Frankle, *The Perpetual Line-Up: Unregulated Police Face Recognition in America*, Georgetown Law, Center on Privacy & Technology, October 18, 2016.

8 IEEE, *Ethically Aligned Design*, First Edition (2019).

9 For a more extensive discussion of these principles, see Chapter 8 of *EAD1e* (the chapter of *EAD1e* that focuses on artificial intelligence and the law). The principles served as the basis of discussion at the Law Committee of the 2019 Global Governance of AI Roundtable (GGAR), a multi-stakeholder workshop held in Dubai in conjunction with the World Government Summit. The GGAR Law Committee is pursuing a mandate similar to that of the IEEE's and The Future Society's law committees (the development of norms for the trustworthy adoption of AI-enabled technologies in the legal domain). The author of the current chapter is also chair of the law committee of the 2019 GGAR.

10 An example of a vehicle for obtaining and publicizing such measurements is the series of comparative evaluations conducted by the Text Retrieval Conference (TREC)

under the auspices of the US National Institute of Standards and Technology (NIST). With respect to AI in the service of the law, a legal track within TREC conducted a series of evaluations on the effectiveness of advanced technologies at meeting fact-finding needs typical in US civil proceedings. The studies found considerable variation in the effectiveness of the systems studied, with two systems consistently achieving high scores but others achieving much lower scores (see, e.g., Bruce Hedin, Stephen Tomlinson, Jason R. Baron, and Douglas W. Oard, "Overview of the TREC 2009 Legal Track," in *NIST Special Publication: SP 500-278, The Eighteenth Text Retrieval Conference (TREC 2009) Proceedings (2009)*; also Maura R. Grossman and Gordon V. Cormack, "Technology-Assisted Review in E-Discovery Can Be More Effective and More Efficient Than Exhaustive Manual Review," *Rich JL & Tech* 17 (2010): 1–48). The TREC evaluations have been very valuable in providing empirical data that enabled informed decisions about the adoption of advanced technologies for the purpose of legal fact-finding. There is a need (currently not met) for comparable forums for the evaluation of AI-enabled technologies as applied to other legal tasks.

11  A metric may not, in itself, provide a complete picture of a technology's fitness for purpose; for this reason, quantitative information should be supplemented by qualitative evaluation of the effectiveness of the technology being assessed.

12  The overview, provided in this section, of a process of the institutionalization of norms has benefited from conversations with Scott David at the University of Washington, to whom we give thanks. Any errors in the overview are, of course, ours.

# Chapter 12

# THE CURIOUS CASE OF FAKE NEWS: FIGHTING SMART MACHIAVELLIAN MACHINES

Daniel Lemus-Delgado and Armando López-Cuevas

## The Progress of Fake News

Fake news is everywhere. While this is not a new phenomenon, nowadays technological advances allow the diffusion of fake news in in ways that were unimaginable a few years ago. This reality is changing the traditional ways of doing politics, political culture, and the political system. The fake news problem is not only a question of technology. The root of the problem is the widespread strategy of spreading misinformation and campaigns of disinformation to obtain political power. In other words, the debate is about how a democracy should orient the technology associated with social media to strengthen, and not weaken, the democracy.

For example, Brazil, the largest democracy in Latin America, elected its president in November 2018. The winner was Jair Bolsonaro. Bolsonaro's popularity grew essentially due to the successful disinformation campaign supported by online social media (Belli, 2018). The followers of Bolsonaro created hundreds of WhatsApp groups to share text messages, images, videos, and memes to spread Bolsonaro's misinforming and misleading content against his political rivals (Belli 2018; Bracho-Polanco, 2019). Brazil is just one more case in a series of countries in which fake news scattered by social networks has been a critical element in social life. In India, the spread of false news has unleashed violence in some areas of the country through inflammatory propaganda expanding Hindu nationalism (Mclaughlin, 2018a). WhatsApp, India's most popular messaging platform, has become a vehicle of misinformation in the election (Ponniah, 2019). In Burma, the army has used Facebook as a tool to help with the ethnic cleansing that caused the death of thousands of people (McLaughlin, 2018b). In the United States, misinformation remains a problem for a variety of social networking platforms (Isaac and Roose, 2018).

Recent history shows that the Brexit decision and the triumph of Donald Trump were elections that were won first in the Facebook arena and the rise of Bolsonaro was forged under the shadow of WhatsApp (Nemer, 2018). All these cases evidence how technology interacts with the interests of power groups with the intention of misinforming the population and obtaining favorable results in the electoral process or strengthen a ruler, an ideology, or a political party.

## Machiavelli, Fake News and Democracy

The two major political writings of Niccolò Machiavelli are *The Prince* and *The Discourses on the First Ten Books of Titus Livy* (Ramsay, 2002). In a sense, those influential books, that reflect some aspects of the thought of Machiavelli, founded a political doctrine. In the following centuries Machiavellism, inspired by the work of Machiavelli, won political prestige and justified the use of power to construct strong states without moral considerations. Machiavellism is, in a merely abstract sense, the theory and practice of amoral politics (Scharfstein, 2005).

In this sense, Machiavelli claimed to have one fundamental purpose, to discover how to establish and maintain an independent state in the context of corruption and decadence of Renaissance Italy (Ramsay, 2002). This was in contrast to the political thought of his time that supposed that the monarch was the incarnation of human virtues—justice, magnanimity, pity, and responsibility. Machiavelli proposed a realistic approach to political problems and sketched how the ruler should act (Gilbert, 2006).

In consequence, Machiavelli detached politics from the noblest purposes derived from a Christian perspective of the world and the life of individuals. In a revolutionary approach that challenged the political doctrine of his epoch, Machiavelli considered that monarchs should only focus on human obligations. Thus, the sovereign should build rules of conduct that were not moral rules but rules molded by a realistic and practical view of the political world derived from observing reality and learning from the historical events (Ramsay, 2002).

The idea of human nature reinforced the absence of moral restrictions in the political action. Machiavelli had a deeply pessimistic vision of mankind and its societies. According to Machiavelli, human beings are by nature frail, inconstant, egoistic, and inclined to evil. Therefore, conflicts for wealth, honor, status, and power penetrate and condition the dynamics of all human society. Machiavelli assumed that "human appetites are insatiable, with the result that the human mind is perpetually discontented, and of its few possessions is apt to grow weary" (Rees, 2004: 3).

Without the chains derived from moral obligations, Machiavelli proposed that a ruler should be judged only for his administrative efficiency. A monarch ought to do anything to ensure the survival of the state. According to the circumstances, a ruler could have "sometimes cruelty, sometimes leniency, sometimes loyalty, sometimes villainy" (Gilbert, 2006: 627). Besides, to the extent that the ruler was compelling, the state would be strong and prevail. Therefore, the prosperity of monarch and state is considered to be equal (Gilbert, 2006).

If the human being is naturally evil, the state will always be in constant risk because people first think in an egotistic way, for their self-benefit. Thus, a fundamental threat for all states is that of degeneration and decadence, what Machiavelli denotes the loss of virtue. In other words, each society could become effete and corrupt and, as a consequence, lose the capability to preserve the state (Rees, 2004). In this situation, autocratic rulers may emerge. Under extraordinary circumstances, which require the establishment or rearrangement of the kingdoms, Machiavelli suggested that the best was that one person assumes the mission.

A fundamental precept was that the prince was to manipulating the people through control, manipulation, and influence. A ruler through his leadership and the creation of robust institutions could earn the loyalty of his people and establish his power solidly. Furthermore, controlling people could be a more efficient way to prevent sinister conspiracies. The concept of Machiavelli of the masses was neither democratic nor involved any element of idealization (Rees, 2004). To Machiavelli, the motor that moves the people is the virtue. But this virtue could be molded, oriented, and manipulated through to operate in the masses. The objective of the monarch was that the virtue of each person was congruent with the virtues of the state and the virtues of the ruler. In other words, the monarch, through manipulating the population, pretends that the people renounce their private interests and defend the general interests of the State. Virtues might be implanted or strengthened in a population by the example of great leaders and by the organization of strong institutions, including religious observance, but Machiavelli insists that the most efficacious means of coercing people is by making them terrified of behaving otherwise (Rees, 2004).

From a Machiavellian doctrine, fake news contributes in two ways to consolidate the power of the political actors. The first and the most obvious way is the manipulation of the people. From a Machiavellian perspective, this action is a manner to mold the virtue—the individual and community will of action in the political arena—in the aims to support a strong leader or an autocratic regime. Because political decisions are amoral, they do not limit the use of fake news. The only way to measure its benefits is the effect of reaching its goals. The dissemination of false information, without moral considerations, could only have a unique purpose, to strengthen the state or a man that he could rule most effectively. Fake news is an extraordinary tool to install or preserve autocratic governments and it grows in a land without being scrupulous.

As Punjabi (2017: 429) has noted, the concept of fake news describes "stories that are made up to deceive, stories containing partial truths, stories that are speculative and not based on evidence and stories that we simply do not agree with." Besides, fake news is the construction of deliberate and strategic lies that are presented as news articles and are intended to mislead the public (Seidenberg, 2017). In consequence, fake news is intentionally designed to be ambiguous and manipulate public opinion. Thus, fake news stories tend to be sensationalist, which in turn creates tremendous popular appeal. Moreover, due to their scandalous and often incredible headlines, millions of people consume and share fake news (Watson, 2018).

The power of fake news lies in the fact that it is designed "to exploit quintessential human weaknesses: it appeals to our cynicism, prejudices, and tribal instincts. The cynical, mocking humor that seems to be foundational to contemporary stand-up comedy feeds our expectations that individuals, organizations, and other recognizable entities would actually behave as described by fake news" (Rodgers, 2018: 9).

The use of fake content for political purposes is not new; however, the growing use of Information and Communication Technologies (ICTs) has erased the limits to publishing information in social media at an unprecedented scale, speed, and distance (Guo and Vargo, 2018). At present, social networks have become the main source of how society consumes news and promotes their political identities. Consequently, social media now is a critical tool to influence and manipulate public opinion and political behavior around the world (Alemanno, 2018). Any person can establish a website propagating conspiracy theories or distribute a false story on social media claiming to be real news (Guo and Vargo, 2018).

Fake news weakens democratic basis in three critical ways. First, fake news strengthens the autocratic governments to the extent that it confuses what is true and what is not and this kind of news inhibits a strong vital to government, primarily discrediting the reputation of professional mass media. Second, fake news creates a division between members of the society establishing distrust based on prejudice or sentiment of the ethnic supremacy of one group over others. Finally, as Machiavellianism suggests, fake news is a tool to manipulate the masses and influence the fears of the people. However, in the end, the challenge is more complex. This challenge is about how our societies can safeguard the freedom of thought, belief, and speech, the cornerstones of a democratic society. This challenge is about how we can combat the false news preventing citizens from choosing based on truthful information. And how can the new technologies, like artificial intelligence (AI), contribute to combat the Machiavellian machine of the fake news? It includes not only electoral processes but, in a broader vision, all those forms of thought that go against the basic principles of democracy such as religious discrimination, to mention just one topic.

## AI and Fake News: Two Sides of the Same Coin

This is not the first time AI has aroused global interest and excitement. In the past there have been episodes of AI hype followed by long periods of AI disappointment, known as the AI winter (Buchanan, 2005). Nevertheless, this time it is different due to three main factors:

1. Big data. With an ever more (cyber)-connected world through Internet, online social networks, and Internet of Things (IoT), the amount of digital data grows exponentially. This has allowed us to improve AI algorithms and to combine different sources of data to perform more powerful analytics.
2. Computing power. Moore's Law states that the number of transistors in an electronic chip duplicates approximately every two years, which in turn results in higher computing power. At present, computing power is large and accessible, and technologies such as cloud computing and GPUs have facilitated the processing of Big Data and AI algorithms.
3. Better algorithms. One of the major factors that have influenced the rise in AI excitement is algorithms, especially deep learning algorithms (Bengio, 2009; Goodfellow, 2014; LeCun et al., 2015) that have shown higher performance than traditional machine learning algorithms. Deep learning algorithms for training Artificial Neural Networks are special types of structures that simulate an abstract representation of how the brain learns by means of synapsis and plasticity. Neural networks and the predecessor of deep learning algorithms existed decades ago (LeCun et al., 2015), but it was not until recently that they have outperformed most of the classical machine learning algorithms in almost every task, thanks to the availability of high computing power and Big Data.

AI surrounds us, is everywhere from our smart phones to our transportation systems, the food supply chain, and many other areas. At some proportion, the content we see every day in our streaming services or our web browser is driven in the background by AI algorithms that show a few options for you to choose.

One of the main areas of computer science that has highly benefited from deep learning is natural language processing (NLP), which is the area that studies how to process, understand, and generate human language with computer algorithms (Collobert and Weston, 2008; Young et al., 2018).

With this empowered ability to access, process, understand, and generate information, AI could play opposite roles, that is, two sides of the same coin:

- AI-generated content: Recently, *OpenAI*, a company dedicated to research of AI, declared that they had created an algorithm (GPT-2) to generate human-like text that is so effective that it raises a concern about malicious applications and for that reason they would not release it to the public; instead, they released a smaller version of it (Hern, 2019). Artificially generated content is not a new topic. In fact, several newspapers rely on AI systems to rapidly create snippets of news on different topics or finance (Peiser, 2019); even when an earthquake occurs the *Los Angeles Times* can generate a news report in a matter of seconds.

  Unfortunately, AI algorithms can be used to generate well-articulated convincing fake news. Moreover, AI algorithms can be used to potentiate the propagation of fake news via social network bots. Bots are usually programmed to interact with other bots, forming a so-called *botnet*. These botnets are used to influence users' opinion by injecting messages on social media so as to favor a political figure or to misrepresent that figure's counterparts, for example (García et al., 2014). In addition, some botnets have been programmed to act as a honeypot, attracting people and making them adopt extremist ideologies of terrorism (Garcia et al., 2014; Kramer, 2017; Mostrous, 2018; Varol et al., 2017).

  Fake news generated by AI becomes even more dangerous due to a technique called "style transfer" that allows supplanting any face in a video with another face in a very realistic manner (Johnson et al., 2016; Gatys et al., 2016). This technique, for example, could allow us to create videos of people passing themselves off as political figures or leaders communicating fake news. A different algorithm allows us to generate completely new, realistic faces that could be used to pass as real persons in social networks to propagate fake news.

- AI for the detection of fake news: It is estimated that there are 48 million bot accounts only in Twitter, which represents approximately 15 percent of all active user accounts (Varol et al., 2017). The proportion of these accounts spreading fake news is not clear. Although there are a number of bot detection methods reported in the literature (Cresci et al., 2016 Iqbal et al., 2016; Perera et al., 2013; Taneja et al., 2015; Yang et al., 2013), there are fewer reports on algorithms for the detection of fake news. For an excellent review of algorithms to detect bots, please refer to Loyola-González, et. al. (2019).

As reported by Grinberg (2019), during the 2016 US elections there was a proliferation of fake news. Twitter accounted for 6 percent of all fake news consumption. Interestingly, the fact is that only 1 percent of users were exposed to 80 percent of fake news and 0.1 percent of users were responsible for sharing 80 percent of fake news (perhaps a botnet).

Facebook and Twitter has hardened their policies in relation to the content that you can post on their platforms. Twitter, for example, has enforced several restrictions on the use of its application program interface (API). Facebook has already implemented a feature for users to flag fake news on the site (Mosseri, 2017). Furthermore, Facebook has AI that can detect artificially generated faces and covers these with masks.

By using AI methods, algorithms can be used to identify potential fake news based on the intrinsic patterns of the text and several other attributes like the source of the news, the date when it was posted, the platforms where it was published, and the interactions between users who reacted to these news, among many others.

In general, methods for identifying fake news and bot accounts in social networks can be divided into two: *supervised methods* and *unsupervised methods*.

*Supervised Methods:* These methods use supervised machine learning that consists of training an algorithm on a set of examples (news) already labeled as belonging to a specific class: in this case, fake-news class or real-news class. The algorithms are fed with thousands of labeled examples of news and they learn the intrinsic patterns of the different classes in order to identify which news is fake and which is real. Once the algorithm training is completed, it can be used to identify new news—news content (Wang, 2017), user profiles (Castillo et al., 2011), message propagation (Wu, 2018), and social contexts (Ma et al., 2015). The main problem with this approach is the need of a dataset that is already labeled by humans, that is, they require a reliable human pre-annotated dataset to train a classification model. Some of the methods used here are support vector machines, deep neural networks, random forest, among others.

*Unsupervised Methods:* These methods do not need a dataset of labeled examples; instead they cluster news based on similarity of their attributes (Shu, 2017; Yang et al., 2019). Rubin et al. (2015) have used gCLUTO (Graphical CLUstering TOolkit) clustering package to help differentiate news reports based on the similarity of the based on chosen clustering algorithm. This method involves running a large amount of dataset and forming/sorting a small number of clusters using agglomerative clustering with the k-nearest neighbor approach, clustering similar news reports based on the normalized frequency of relations.

In both types of methods there are common features that are relevant to the correct identification of fake news.

- Linguistic factors such as the frequency of unigrams (words) and bigrams (pairs of words) are extracted from the collection of words in a story to perform statistical analysis or classification with a Bag of words or TF-IDF techniques. The use of punctuation can help the fake news detection algorithm to differentiate between deceptive and truthful texts (Parikh and Atrey, 2018). Other types of features used to detect fake news are the *psycholinguistic features* such as the sentiment or dimension of emotions in the text or part-of-speech (POS) category (e.g., articles, verbs). Another attribute in the text used by the algorithms are the *named-entity-recognition*, which consist of detecting commonly known entities such as countries, companies, or political figures. Readability metrics, such as Flesch–Kincaid, are also used for classification of news. As stated in Yang et al. (2018) the lexical diversity and cognition of the deceivers are totally different from the truth teller.
- Image factors. Beyond the text information, images in fake news are also different from that in real news. Cartoon-like low-resolution images and irrelevant images are frequently observed in fake news.
- Network factors. The network structure and behaviors are also important features used to identify fake news. As stated in Yang et al. (2018) the methods based on the knowledge graph analysis can achieve 61–95 percent accuracy. Another promising research direction is exploiting the social network behavior to identify the deception.

## Technology Is Fundamental, but It Is Not Enough

Fake news negatively impacts some of the most essential principles of the liberal order. In some ways, fake news has become an art practiced and accepted as a necessary part of election campaigns and political debates. However, this can have a negative impact on democratic values such as liberty, equality, justice, truth, and diversity. As explained above, Fake News Detection is an achievable technical problem. But AI approaches alone are not sufficient to solve the problem. Technology only or human collaboration alone will be indispensable. It is essential to strengthen institutions that promote basic values that allow a culture of democracy to combat the false news. In this sense, the most important is political will and public demand to make it happen.

Thus, AI could play an essential role in assisting to detect suspicious news on the web, a task that if done only by humans could become infeasible due to the large amount of data. However, fake news detection is a highly complex task given that it involves knowledge of the context of the news. One possible scenario could be that an AI system selects putative fake news based on different patterns and a multidisciplinary group of people decide whether that selected news is fake or not. On the contrary, in the not too distant future, the power of fake news and the technologies associated with its expansion will be the most important tool to determine the political life of our societies. And stories like those of Trump or Bolsonaro will be the norm and not the exception.

In this sense, if we want to democratic values prevail tomorrow, we need to take concrete actions today with the intention of stopping the fake news. As explained above, fake news detection is an achievable technical difficult. The critical problem concerns social and cultural issues. The big question is how we can strengthen democracy in times of populism, lies, xenophobia, and economic and social polarization. In some ways, the expansion of fake news is a consequence of an art practiced and accepted as a necessary part of election campaigns and political debates. Thus, this way of thinking narrowly resembles Machiavelli's famous quote: "the ends justify the means." Even some politicians with "good intentions" could be tempted to utilize these mechanisms to win the elections that allow them to launch their respectable or morally superior projects.

If we want to enclose fake news, we need a political will and public demand. Specifically, we need to develop critical thinking not only in schools and universities but also among ordinary citizens promoting the use of verified data in public campaigns. Also, it is necessary to establish specific obligations among the mass media about the criteria to verify the information that they communicate.

Moreover, it is indispensable the establishment of a framework that compels the companies of social networks that clearly warn us about the people or companies behind that financing of the social media accounts and what informative services are paid.

Besides, we need to create citizen advisory councils to audit the quality of the information published on the network and we must demand the foundation of autonomous mechanisms for verifying candidate and political parties information. Finally, we suggest that future research problems in the field of fake news should be two objectives. First, the development of more accurate algorithms to identify, track, and even warn sites that generate fake news. Second, the recognition of best practices to encourage citizens to be thoughtful about the information they read and to have a proactive attitude to demand campaigns based on correct and precise information and choose candidates to stay away from fake news.

## References

Alemanno, A. (2018). How to Counter Fake News? A Taxonomy of Anti-fake News Approaches. *European Journal of Risk Regulation*, 9(1): 1–5. doi: https://doi.org/10.1017/err.2018.12.

Belli, L. (2018). WhatsApp skewed Brazilian election, proving social media's danger to democracy. *The Conversation*. Retrieved from: https://theconversation.com/whatsapp-skewed-brazilian-election-proving-social-medias-danger-to-democracy-106476.

Bengio, Y. (2009). Learning Deep Architectures for AI. *Foundations and Trends in Machine Learning*, 2(1): 1–127. doi: 10.1561/2200000006.

Bracho-Polanco, E. (2019). How Jair Bolsonaro used "fake news" to win power. *SBS News*. Retrieved from: https://www.sbs.com.au/news/dateline/how-jair-bolsonaro-used-fake-news-to-win-power.

Buchanan, B. G. (2005). A (Very) Brief History of Artificial Intelligence. *AI Magazine*, 26(4): 53–60.

Castillo, C., Mendoza, M., and Poblete, B. (2011). Information credibility on twitter. *Proceedings of the 20th International Conference on World Wide Web*, pp. 675–84. ACM.

Collobert, R., and Weston, J. (2008). A unified architecture for natural language. *Proceedings of the 25th International Conference on Machine Learning*, pp. 160–67. doi: https://doi.org/10.1609/aimag.v26i4.1848.

Cresci, S., Di Pietro, R., Petrocchi, M., Spognardi, A., and Tesconi, M. (2016). DNA-Inspired Online Behavioral Modeling and Its Application to Spambot Detection. *IEEE Intelligent Systems*, 31(5): 58–64.

García, S., Grill, M., Stiborek, J., and Zunino, A. (2014). An Empirical Comparison of Botnet Detection Methods. *Computers & Security*, 45: 100–23. doi: https://doi.org/10.1016/j.cose.2014.05.011.

Gatys, L., Ecker, A., and Bethge, M. (2016). Image style transfer using convolutional neural networks. *Proceedings of the IEEE Conference on Computer Vision and Pattern Recognition*, pp. 2414–23. Retrieved from: https://www.cv-foundation.org/openaccess/content_cvpr_2016/papers/Gatys_Image_Style_Transfer_CVPR_2016_paper.pdf.

Gilbert, F. (2006). Machiavelli, Niccolò (1469–1527). In D. M. Borchert (ed.), *Encyclopedia of Philosophy*, pp. 626–29. Detroit, MI: Macmillan.

Goodfellow, I., Pouget-Abadie, J., Mirza, M., Xu, B., Warde-Farley, D., Ozair, S., Courville, A., and Bengio, Y. (2014). NIPS'14: Proceedings of the 27th International Conference on Neural Information Processing Systems, Vol. 2, pp. 2672–80.

Grinberg, N., Joseph, K., Friedland, L., Swire-Thompson, B., and Lazer, D. (2019). Fake News on Twitter during the 2016 US Presidential Election. *Science*, 363(6425): 374–78.

Guo, L., and Vargo, C. (2018) "Fake News" and Emerging Online Media Ecosystem: An Integrated Intermedia Agenda-Setting Analysis of the 2016 U.S. Presidential Election. *Communication Research*, 1–23. doi: https://0-doi-org.millenium.itesm.mx/10.1177/0093650218777177.

Hern, A. (2019). New AI fake text generator may be too dangerous to release, say creators. *The Guardian*. Retrieved from: https://www.theguardian.com/technology/2019/feb/14/elon-musk-backed-ai-writes-convincing-news-fiction.

Iqbal, M. S., Zulkernine, M., Jaafar, F., and Fcfraud, Y. Gu. (2016). Fighting clickfraud from the user side. *17th International Symposium on High Assurance Systems Engineering (HASE)*, pp. 157–64.

Isaac, M., and Roose, K. (2018). Disinformation spreads on WhatsApp ahead of Brazilian election. *New York Times*. Retrieved from: https://www.nytimes.com/2018/10/19/technology/whatsapp-brazil-presidential-election.html.

Johnson, J., Alahi, A., and Fei-Fei, L. (2016). Perceptual Losses for Real-Time Style Transfer and Super-Resolution. *European Conference on Computer Vision*. doi: 10.1007/978-3-319-46475-6_43.

Kramer, S. (2017). Identifying viral bots and cyborgs in social media. Retrieved from: https://www.oreilly.com/ideas/identifying-viral-bots-and-cyborgs-in-social-media.

LeCun, Y., Bengio, Y., and Hinton, G. (2015). Deep Learning. *Nature*, 521: 436–44. doi: 10.1038/nature14539.

Loyola-González, O., Monroy, R., Rodríguez, J. López-Cuevas, A. and Mata-Sánchez, J. (2019). Contrast pattern-based classification for Bot detection on Twitter. *IEEE Access* 7(1), 18. doi: 10.1109/ACCESS.2019.2904220.

Ma, J., Gao, W., Wei, Z., Lu, Y., and Wong, K.-F. (2015). Detect rumors using time series of social context information on microblogging websites. *Proceedings of the 24th ACM International on Conference on Information and Knowledge Management*, pp. 1751–54. ACM.

Mclaughlin, T. (2018a). Disinformation is spreading on WhatsApp in India. Retrieved from: https://www.theatlantic.com/international/archive/2018/09/fighting-whatsapp-disinformation-india-kerala-floods/569332/.

McLaughlin, T. (2018b). How Facebook's rise fueled chaos and confusion in Myanmar. *Wired*. Retrieved from: https://www.wired.com/story/how-facebooks-rise-fueled-chaos-and-confusion-in-myanmar/.

Mosseri, A. (2017). News feed fyi: Addressing hoaxes and fake news, August 2017 [online]. Available: https://newsroom.fb.com/news/2016/12/news-feed-fyi-addressing-hoaxes-and-fake-news/.

Mostrous, A. (2018). Anatomy of an Investigation. *British Journalism Review*, 29(2): 14–18. doi: https://doi.org/10.1177/0956474818781155.

Nemer, D. (2018). The three types of WhatsApp users getting Brazil's Jair Bolsonaro elected. *The Guardian*. Retrieved from: https://www.theguardian.com/world/2018/oct/25/brazil-president-jair-bolsonaro-whatsapp-fake-news.

Parikh, S. B., and Atrey, P. K. (2018). Media-Rich Fake News Detection: A Survey. *2018 IEEE Conference on Multimedia Information Processing and Retrieval (MIPR)*, Miami, FL, pp. 436–41.

Peiser, J. (2019). The rise of the robot reporter. *New York Times*. Retrieved from: https://www.nytimes.com/2019/02/05/business/media/artificial-intelligence-journalism-robots.html.

Perera, K. S., Neupane, B., Faisal, M. A., Aung, Z., and Woon, W. L. (2013). A novel ensemble learning-based approach for click fraud detection in mobile advertising. In R. Prasath and T. Kathirvalavakumar (eds.), *Mining Intelligence and Knowledge Exploration*, pp. 370–82, Cham: Springer.

Ponniah, K. (2019). WhatsApp: The "black hole" of fake news in India's election. *BBC News*. Retrieved from: https://www.bbc.com/news/world-asia-india-47797151.

Punjabi, P. (2017). Science and the "Fake News" Conundrum. *Perfusion*, 32(6): 429.

Ramsay, M. (2002). Machiavelli (1469–1527). In A. Edwards and J. Townshend (eds.), *Interpreting Modern Political Philosophy*, pp. 21–40. Basingstoke, Hampshire: Palgrave Macmillan.

Rees, E. A. (2004). *Political Thought from Machiavelli to Stalin*. Basingstoke, Hampshire: Palgrave Macmillan.

Rodgers, M. L. (2018). Fake News: A New Enemy of Learning. *The National Teaching & Learning Forum*, 27(4): 9–11.

Rubin, V. L., Conroy, N. J., and Chen, Y. (2015). "Towards news verification: Deception detection methods for news discourse," Hawaii International Conference on System Sciences.

Scharfstein, B. A. (2005). Machiavellism. In M. C. Horowitz (ed.), *New Dictionary of the History of Ideas*, pp. 1325–28. Detroit, MI: Charles Scribner's Sons.

Seidenberg, S. (2017). Lies and Libel: Fake News Lacks Straightforward Cure. *ABA Journal*, July 2017. Retrieved from: http://www.abajournal.com/magazine/article/fake_news_libel_law/history_fake_news.

Shu, K., Sliva, A., Wang, S., Tang, J., and Liu, H. (2017). Fake News Detection on Social Media: A Data Mining Perspective. *ACM SIGKDD Explorations Newsletter*, 19(1): 22–36.

Taneja, M., Garg, K., Purwar, A., and Sharma, S. (2015). Prediction of click frauds in mobile advertising. *Eighth International Conference on Contemporary Computing (IC3)*, volume 1 pp. 162–66.

Varol, O., Ferrara, E., Davis, C. A., Menczer, F., and Flammini, A. (2017). Online human-bot interactions: Detection, estimation, and characterization. *Paper presented at the Proceedings of the International AAAI Conference on Web and Social Media (ICWSM)*, Montreal, Canada. Retrieved from: https://www.aaai.org/ocs/index.php/ICWSM/ICWSM17/paper/view/15587/14817.

Wang, W. Y. (2017). "Liar, liar pants on fire": A new benchmark dataset for fake news detection. arXiv preprint arXiv:1705.00648.

Watson, C. (2018). Information Literacy in a Fake/False News World: An Overview of the Characteristics of Fake News and Its Historical Development. *International Journal of Legal Information*, 46(2): 93–96.

Wu, L., and Liu, H. (2018). Tracing fake-news footprints: Characterizing social media messages by how they propagate. *Proceedings of the Eleventh ACM International Conference on Web Search and Data Mining (WSDM)*, pp. 637–45. ACM.

Yang, C., Harkreader, R., and Gu, G. (2013). Empirical Evaluation and New Design for Fighting Evolving Twitter Spammers. *IEEE Transactions on Information Forensics and Security*, 8(8): 1280–93.

Yang, S., Shu, K., Wang, S., Gu, R., Wu, F., and Liu, H. (2019). Unsupervised fake news detection on social media: A generative approach. *Proceedings of 33rd AAAI Conference on Artificial Intelligence*. Retrieved from: http://www.public.asu.edu/~skai2/files/aaai_2019_unsupervised.pdf.

Yang, Y., Zheng, L., Zhang, J., Cui, Q., Li, Z., and Yu, P. S. (2018). TI-CNN: Convolutional neural networks for fake news detection. arXiv preprint arXiv:1806.00749.

Young, T., Hazarika, D., Poria, S., and Cambria, E. (2018). Recent Trends in Deep Learning Based Natural Language Processing. *IEEE Computational Intelligence Magazine*, 13(3): 55–75. doi: 10.1109/MCI.2018.2840738.

# Chapter 13

# APPLICATIONS OF ARTIFICIAL INTELLIGENCE AND RPA TO IMPROVE GOVERNMENT PERFORMANCE

Luis Soto and Sergio Biggemann

Technological development within information technology has permeated all areas of business and types of institutions; public institutions have not been the exception. Most applications of artificial intelligence (AI), machine learning, or robotic process automation (RPA)[1] have been developed with commercial applications in mind. However, governments worldwide have also been working on applications of AI aiming to improve their service levels to their citizens (see Figure 13.1).

As opposed to an Orwellian, big brother approach (Orwell, 1949) that makes governments look like wanting to take advantage of technology to control their citizens, this chapter takes a customer service approach to explore the most likely applications that governments are developing to improve customer service. Three different examples have been selected.

From the several applications of intelligent automation health care is prominent. Kalis et al. (2018) find that robot-assisted technology is one application in this area with a potential annual value of $40 billion. This application lies on the RPA category; nevertheless, other applications such as administrative workflow ($18 billion) and fraud detection ($17 billion) are more on the thinking side of intelligent automation. It is in these applications that we have been able to identify real examples of AI applications in government settings, which we describe using a customer service interactionist mindset.

When a person (customer) approaches a government institution seeking for a service, for the service experience to occur, the parties need to engage in interaction; one party acts and the other re-acts. The customer request is an act that the service provider first needs to make sense of. That is, the service provider interprets the request and responds accordingly; the customer construes

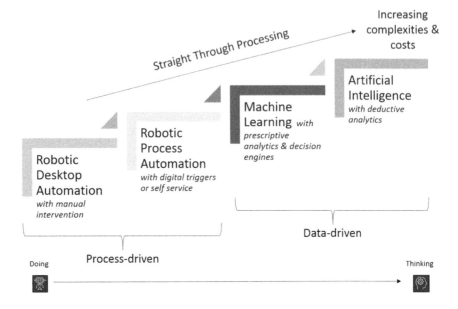

**Figure 13.1** Intelligent automation.
*Source*: https://medium.com/@cfb_bots/the-difference-between-robotic-process-automation-and-artificial-intelligence-4a71b4834788.

the response and depending on the meaning it has given to the response, the customer responds. This exchange of acts continues for as long as the parties understand the other acts and the service experience is completed. Norms of interaction develop over time. The parties build a relationship and learn how to make sense of the other party's action and how to respond. Fundamental to relationship development is that one party trusts and considers the other party committed. Thus, interaction occurs within the context of relationship and is guided by the parties' previous experiences and expectation of the future. Although the service is provided by the organization, the customer construes the service encounter in the context of the relationship between him/her and the person at the organizational frontline. Thus, s(he) assesses whether the person is trustworthy and seems to be committed to solve his/her problems.

The next section describes examples of AI applications of government services.

Administrative workflow and customer information, not necessarily for fraud detection but instead to make sure that customers' information and needs are correct, have been driving AI initiatives among governments in several countries. For instance, Australia has been using digital customer service agents for providing public welfare services. Algorithms are used to help the government agencies in making benefits' decisions through the application of complex rules calculating eligibility and payment levels (Nili et al., 2019). Digital agents are found to operate at three different levels. Nili et al. (2019) stress that it could be a basic triage: one application where customers are guided to the right service for their needs by a digital agent using natural language processing; another, more complex application could be targeted assistance, such as auto-filling forms for customers based on their profile; and the most complex application could be proactive assistance, where digital agents using predictive analytics recommend future services to customers based on events that will occur in the future, such as giving birth, getting married, or retiring. These digital agents continually learn from customers' interactions.

In a similar situation (i.e., providing assistance), the Accident Compensation Corporation (ACC) in New Zealand, whose mission is to prevent injuries and get New Zealanders and visitors back to everyday life if they've had an accident,[2] receives two million claims per year, 96 percent of which are accepted. ACC has started using predictive analytics with the objective of improving the claim registration and approval process. Due to the public character of ACC, the development of an algorithm to deal with accident claims had been restricted in its application to fast track the easy, rather straightforward claims and continues to require human intervention for the complex claims. Algorithms, capable of identifying features of a claim relevant to a claim that would be accepted, were created using 12 million claims received over the past six years. The system only accepts claims. If the system recommends to reject a claim, the intervention of a human who reassesses the claim is also required.

New Zealand's tax department has recently announced a very ambitious use of AI. They have started trials of a $1.9 billion project aiming for making life easier for businesses and individuals. The robo-taxman will be hunting down cash jobs using big data analytics to spot anomalies and detect noncompliance. Like in the previous cases, sophisticated algorithms are expected to use third party's data to compare with businesses' and individuals' tax declarations. The system has not been deployed yet, it is only on trial phase, but prophets, gurus, and pundits are already explaining why this is inconvenient for people. The critical assumption is that the system will not be able to understand that not every worker is capable of achieving business standards and may be difficult to argue with the tax office. There is also an assumption about the complexity of the algorithms and the inability of accountants and lawyers to understand those systems, which ultimately will only put taxpayers at a disadvantage.

The first two examples illustrate two applications of AI in public organizations associated with providing services to large numbers of customers needing assistance. The last illustration is not about providing assistance, but controlling people's tax declarations. However, all three share commonalities.

As there is a potential for fraud when a customer applies for a service, digital agents review not only the information contained in the application but also additional information related to the applicant, including information available on social media.[3] However, the use of additional information raises public concerns about privacy as well as misuse of information, or even more serious matters such as the use of wrong information due to mistakes in identification of the customer, which may potentially occur despite advances of face recognition technology, to mention one. This is exacerbated with the fact that the tax office has already announced that they are not obliged to declare where they have captured the information its robo-taxman is going to use.

Other types of applications are more commonly found in developing countries where keeping accurate records of people such as identification documents or addresses require cumbersome procedures. Although information technology permits electronic storage of information, decreasing the chances of misplacing people's identification documents, compared to using folders as it was in the past, the level of accuracy of information is still limited; thus, more advanced technology has been used to solve these problems. We present here an example of AI applications to improve the processes of identification in Bolivia.

The Law for Digital Citizenship recently sanctioned in Bolivia put this country at the leading edge of regulation for digital identity as well as for digital documents. All public entities must now issue digital credentials for all the services and registries; however, the level of institutionalization of most agencies is very low and, thus, moving toward digitalization has been challenging. Paper-based documents are commonly used and there is no existing ecosystem or network for creating digital credentials and to check their validity to verify any application. A case on the use of AI and RPA is presented here to illustrate how digital credentials are issued to comply with the new Bolivian law in the verification and revision of paper-based documents and how they are converted into digital verified credentials.

The country requires all its male citizens to comply with a compulsory one-year military service before their 23rd birthday. However, for diverse reasons, a significant number of people do not comply with this requirement and thus must request a redemption card in replacement of the military service certificate, which government institutions and universities require for job applications or to enroll for studies. Banks also require this document to process loan applications. The old process to obtain a redemption card was manual and could take from three to six months to complete, requiring many interactions with the Ministry of Defence, which ultimately validates the documents and issues the credential or rejects the application. Several documents were required, starting with a letter to the minister of defense requesting the redemption credential and including the applicant's birth certificate issued with the new seal,[4] the applicant's identification card, not expired, a medical certificate for blood type and indication of any disability, the applicant's driver's license (optional), a professional diploma or university degree (optional), a photograph with the card number (LM + year of birth – ID number – current year), and a bank deposit for the amount of Bs 4,000[5] plus 5 percent for each year after the 23rd birthday of the applicant.

In the old workflow (Figure 13.2), once the applicant has lodged the application accompanied with all these documents, a clerk from the Ministry of Defence reviews each document and, if in doubt, contacts the issuer to validate the information. The officer can request in the process additional information

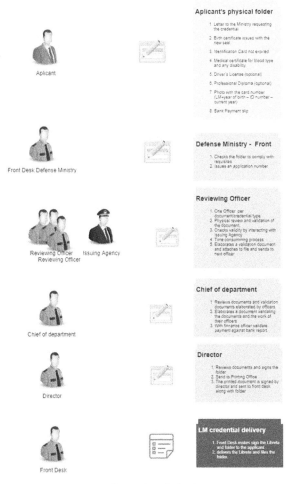

**Figure 13.2** Old workflow.

from the applicant if s(he) deems it necessary. Once the documents have been verified, a report is written to the director who passes the reviewed file to the section's chief for a final decision to issue (or not) the redemption credential to the applicant. If the credential is approved, the service typically provides the individual with a document—a credential—that can be used to prove that the person has complied with the requisites of the military service. The whole process is not only expensive but extremely inefficient and time consuming.

To address these inefficiencies, a new digital platform based on AI and RPA was designed (Figure 13.3). The Ministry of Defence signed agreements with the National Service of Identification, the Civil Registry Service, and banks

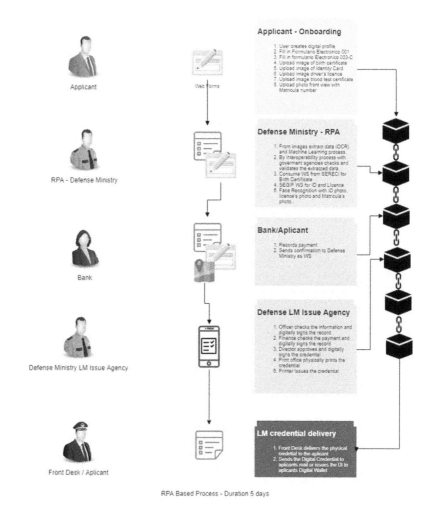

**Figure 13.3** New workflow.

to create a Web Services Interoperability Network (WSIN) so each agency will validate their documents. WSIN has the following architecture: (1) cloud-based solution, (2) face recognition user authentication, (3) optical character recognition, (4) image recognition, (5) microservices, (6) ecosystem of trusted agencies, (7) interoperability web services, and (8) permissioned blockchain.

As the law requires the documents to be validated by the issuer, this system is designed so the issuer himself/herself does the validation, with no previous request by the Ministry of Defence. The applicant uploads all the documents as images, including the photo with the number and enrolls his face for authentication. Then the former manual validation process is replaced by a robotic process with the help of Machine Learning and Vision Imaging functions, which depend on the type of documents and its contents. For instance, the identity card has two sides: at the front there is a photograph, a fingerprint, the person's signature, and the ID number. At the back the card contains the bio data and person's address. The process of information extraction and validation extracts all the components from the front and classifies them as image or characters. The numbers and series are recognized and saved. From the back all the information is extracted and classified, and the information is presented to the user for validation and acceptance. With the accepted information and the images, a JSON object is built, and the Identification Agency has a web service to validate the information. If the answer is positive the next document is processed, else the application is rejected and the user is informed.

The birth certificate is printed only on one side and includes a QR code. From the image all the information is extracted and classified and saved. The QR code is decoded and saved. The information is presented to the user for validation, and the digital data is validated through the Interoperability service provided by the Civil Registry Service. The photograph is processed to comply with red background, front face, and number according to codification. A comparison and biometric validation between the photograph from the ID card and face enrolment is performed. If there is an issue, the user is informed, he can correct and resubmit the photograph. If the problem persists, the application is redirected to the manual process. The driver's license has information on the front and back. It has a photograph, from which information is extracted and saved together with the rest of the text that includes name and other personal information of the applicant. It has a QR code at the back, from which information is extracted. Then, the information is presented to the applicant for validation and acceptance, the photograph is biometrically compared with the other photographs. : If there is an issue, the user is informed and given the choice of accepting the application with the flagged item of withdraw it, because the document is optional. For diplomas and work certificates the information is extracted and classified by name, institution, degree, and work designation and also dates and the photograph processes, if any. The information is saved and presented to the user for validation and acceptance. If there are more documents of this type, they are processed and saved to the electronic file. If all the information contained in the application passes the validation, the system issues a code and calculates the amount the applicant has to pay. The applicant pays at the bank, the payment is registered, and the system builds a document with photograph and all the validated information. This document is the redemption card that has to be digitally signed by the director; the document is printed and a notification to the user is mailed. The document is sent to the agency front desk and made available to the applicant.

This solution is equipped with an algorithm that learns about the issues with documents and makes modifications to the system, which are consistent with the problem-solving processes applied when human intervention was required, thus continuing to reduce the processing time while increasing the accuracy of the process. The final decision about issuing the certificate of redemption, which was earlier made by the section's chief, is now taken by the algorithm that uses a combination of the documents reviewed and the reasons that the individual alleges for having failed to complete the military service. Thus the digitalization of documents and automation of processes deliver significant benefits, having reduced the time for an application to be processed from three to six months to only a couple of days. The system also creates a digital validated file, the individual's true identity that could be later used for all identification processes.

In conclusion, the previous three examples of AI application in a government services context are, on the one hand, different from one another and suited to illustrate the diversity of applications that this technology allows for; on the other, they share the fact that they have not been designed with the intention to improve the customer experience in mind. Although the outcomes might improve the customers' experience, the fact that this appears not to have been the driver for the application design might mean that optimal results are yet to be achieved. For improving the customer's experience, the customer's engagement with the service provider is fundamental. Vivek et al. (2012) argue that engagement requires trust and commitment. In an interaction, trust enables the parties to take risks, providing the grounds on which the parties stand with some level of certainty that the other will not act opportunistically and that the other has the competence to deliver, is honest, or is benevolent toward its counterpart (Doney and Cannon, 1997; Mayer et al., 1995). Also, for a customer to actively engage, the other party's commitment matters. That is, a customer would like to see that the service provider is willing to care about the customer's needs (i.e., attitudinal commitment) or has made available limited resources to provide the service (i.e., instrumental commitment) (Gundlach et al., 1995; Wiener, 1982), so the service experience overall is satisfactory. However, in these new forms of service provision, at the organization's frontline it is a robot that interacts with the customer and not a human; thus, a question on how much a customer engages is posed. For the future development of AI applications in government institutions, an inter-actionist approach with focus on customer engagement is recommended.

## Notes

1   Sometimes these names are used interchangeably, we adopt the idea of Intelligent Automation that differentiates RPA as software robot that mimics human actions from AI as the simulation of human intelligence by machines, with machine learning as an intermediate state.
2   Source: https://www.acc.co.nz/about-us/who-we-are/what-we-do/.
3   A classic example would be of someone claiming compensation for a broken leg while posting selfies on the Internet skiing in the Southern Alps.
4   The Bolivian government regularly updates their forms causing the automatic obsoles-cence of any certificates previously issued.
5   Approximately US$580.

## References

Doney, P. M., and Cannon, J. P. (1997). An examination of the nature of trust in buyer–seller relationships. *Journal of Marketing, 61*(2), 35–51.

Gundlach, G. T., Achrol, R. S., and Mentzer, J. T. (1995). The structure of commitment in exchange. *Journal of Marketing, 59*(1), 78–92.

Kalis, B., Collier, M., and Fu, R. (2018). 10 promising AI applications in health care. *Harvard Business Review, 96*(May), 1076.

Mayer, R. C., Davis, J. H., and Schoorman, F. D. (1995). An integrative model of organiza-tional trust. *Academy of Management Review, 20*(3), 709–34. doi:10.2307/258792.

Nili, A., Barros, A., and Tate, M. (2019). The public sector can Teach us a lot about digit-izing customer service. *MIT Sloan Management Review, 60*(2), 84–87.

Orwell, G. (1949). *Nineteen Eighty-Four, A novel* (1st American edn). New York: Harcourt, Brace.

Vivek, S. D., Beatty, S. E., and Morgan, R. M. (2012). Customer engagement: Exploring customer relationships beyond purchase. *Journal of Marketing Theory and Practice, 20*(2), 122–46.

Wiener, Y. (1982). Commitment in organizations: A normative view. *Academy of Management Review, 7*(3), 418–28.

# Chapter 14

# CONCLUSION

## J. Mark Munoz and Al Naqvi

The advent of artificial intelligence (AI) is not an ordinary change. In the epic battle between human consciousness shaping the human desire to survive and the forces of nature that constantly inundate human mind with the fears of the unknown, economic revolutions serve as the mediating bridges. Agricultural revolution brought humans out of the jungle, and industrial revolution gave humans the perception of greater control over their surroundings. The information revolution enhanced that aura of control and Internet provided a sense of collective consciousness. Our fears and aspirations became shared and collective.

While revolutionary in similar respects as the ones just pointed out, this new era of machines is unlike what we have ever seen before. In all previous revolutions, machines were subservient to humans. Whether a plow in a farmer's hands, or the car's steering wheel, or a program running in a computer, machines did what humans wanted and expected them to do. That is not the case anymore. In this revolution however, there is a clear path to a shared future between machines and humans—a future that humans have never prepared for. The AI era therefore requires a new sense of humbleness and curiosity as never undertaken before. It requires a new level of collective consciousness.

By all indications this is the defining moment for the human civilization. It is when humankind must recognize the gravity of the situation. From the government perspective, there is grave responsibility. In fact, a century from now, if humankind makes it that far, the historians will look back at today's governments to observe what was done right and what went wrong. The central message of this book is to "plan." This book is about planning the course of human civilization to embrace and understand the revolutionary dynamics of the AI revolution and then implement those plans.

The dynamics of this revolution are powerful. We need to plan, we need to have a strategy, we need to have awareness, and we need to have a clear path forward for the entire humankind. From designing the structural dynamics of the revolution in a country to managing unemployment, retraining, and reskilling the population, this book gives a clear path to make AI a national and an international success. There are times when the book seems to take a rather gloomy posture (e.g., unemployment), but that is only to ensure that if we are to err in certain key aspects of managing the economy (e.g., unemployment) let's do so on the end of being superconservative versus operating in denial and finding half the world unemployed. We observed a similar scenario unfold in the American Midwest when mechanical automation led to major plant shutdowns and significant rise in unemployment. The cautionary tone of this book is an invitation to plan more aggressively.

We can say with no sense of eagerness or embellishment that the most important role of any government today has become the management of the AI revolution. If you do it well, your country and the world have a promising future. If not, the implications are unthinkable.

The chapters in this book suggest that AI and robotic process automation (RPA) impact technological development, employment, economy, security, and the operations of government worldwide.

In the featured chapters, five themes are evident:

**Rapid changes**. Technological innovation is shaping and will continue to shape company and government dynamics. This requires organizations to quickly absorb and respond to changes taking place.

**Adaptation is essential**. Organizations need to constantly adapt and reinvent themselves in order to respond to industry, market, and competitive changes taking place.

**Technology stimulates growth**. There are countless benefits ascribed to AI and RPA. Organizations that cultivate and nurture these technologies can gain an advantage.

**Challenges abound**. There are numerous challenges to deal with in regard to AI and RPA. These challenges range from technology absorption, job losses, need for skills update, security, and even ethics.

**Strategic, proactive planning is beneficial**. Organizational changes do not take place overnight. Understanding organizational capabilities well and carefully planning for future steps is imperative.

The profound impact of AI and RPA on governments will likely linger into the future. AI will contribute an estimated $15.7 Trillion to the global economy by 2030 and will boost GDP of local economies by approximately 26 percent (PWC, 2016). Unprecedented technological breakthroughs will take many organizations into uncharted waters, thereby challenging conventional wisdom. AI is predicted to be driving trucks by 2027, writing best-selling novels by 2049, and replacing surgeons by 2053 (Gray, 2017).

Meanwhile, many companies and governments are ill prepared for the changes brought about by AI and RPA. Only about 20 percent of organizations possess essential skills to succeed with AI technology (Rao, 2017).

Effective strategy can be a game changer for companies and governments worldwide. Strategic AI approaches that can be helpful to organizations include (1) assessing opportunities and weighing in on technology, competitive pressures, and pain points, (2) determining key priorities, (3) ensuring resources relating to talent, culture, and technology are in place, and (4) planning for proper governance and control with trust and transparency in mind (PWC, 2016).

Table 14.1 shows the five phases in which governments need to respond.

**Table 14.1** Phases for AI and RPA integration for governments' phase agenda action plan

| Phase 1 | Assessment and evaluation | Assess where organization is with regard to AI and RPA in terms of technology and organizational competencies; evaluate challenges and opportunities; identify needs |
| --- | --- | --- |
| Phase 2 | Development of AI/RPA strategic plan | Create a strategic plan for the successful AI/RPA implementation; engage multiple stakeholders in the planning process; align with mission and goals |
| Phase 3 | Resource alignment and prioritization | Weigh in on resource availability, manpower competency, technological access as well as market and competitive factors; prioritize action agenda; establish timelines |
| Phase 4 | Implementation of plan | Identify key people who will put the plan into action; implement in stages and provide opportunities for assessment and evaluation; provide room for flexibility in order to respond to disruptive innovation and unforeseen market changes |
| Phase 5 | Review and refine | Review and refine the AI/RPA strategic plan periodically |

As shown in Table 14.1, the process of utilizing AI/RPA within the government framework would take time and require advance planning. Table 14.2 highlights key components and considerations of the strategic plan for governments.

**Table 14.2** Outline of the strategic AI/RPA plan for governments' topic considerations

| | |
|---|---|
| Vision and mission | Identify what your goals are with regard to AI/RPA and how these align with the government's vision and mission. |
| Market research | Conduct research on technological and industry trends, market demands, as well as the competitive landscape. |
| Organization, people, and operational considerations | Prepare an analysis on what changes will take place in the organizational structure, manpower resources, and operational structure as AI/RPA plans are implemented. |
| Economic issues | Assess the impact of AI/RPA plans on the economy. |
| Sociocultural and domestic political issues | Assess how the AI/RPA plan will impact the citizenry as well as domestic politics and policy implementation. |
| Technological factors | Identify technological resources in AI/RPA that are needed to accomplish AI/RPA plans. |
| Financial management | Conduct a cost and benefit analysis of the plan. Assess the overall costs and financial impact of the AI/RPA plan. |
| Marketing and public relations | Outline marketing and public relations initiatives that need to be conducted in connection with the AI/RPA plans. |
| Geopolitical and geoeconomic considerations | Evaluate the geopolitical as well as geoeconomic impact of the AI/RPA plans, specifically, how the plans will affect the government's relationship with other countries. |
| Implementation schedule and timeline | Indicate a clear set of action agenda as well as the timelines of implementation of the AI/RPA plan. |
| Impact of the plan | Outline key transformation that will take place in the country as a result of the AI/RPA plan. |
| Future trends, risks, challenges, and opportunities | Assess future trends, risks, challenges, and opportunities relating to the implementation of the AI/RPA plan. Provide contingency plans. |

Table 14.2 underscores the fact that governments need to consider numerous factors to effectively plan for a successful AI/RPA strategy. A high level of commitment, mission congruency, and intentionality can make all the difference. Mehr (2017) identified the need for governments to: (1) incorporate AI in their goals, (2) engage the citizenry, (3) build on existing resources, (4) consider data preparation, (5) manage ethical risks, and (6) strengthen employee potential.

Furthermore, finding a balance between technological advances and the overall betterment of society is key. A high regard for ethics is essential. The convergence of AI and ethics is critical in the future (Lufkin, 2017).

Governments worldwide are experiencing the influencing forces brought about by AI/RPA. Ultimately, the successes and failures of governments, as well as our society, rest on the level of strategic planning they take and the courses of action they decide upon.

In conclusion, the authors underscore the important message communicated in the book about developing a country's AI strategy. Developing a country's strategy requires three types of planning activities. A government plays three roles: adopter, enabler, and governance. In the adopter role, the government implements AI technologies in both military and nonmilitary government agencies. This happens at all levels of the government–including federal, state, and city level. In the enabler role, a government helps develop and enable innovation in the private sector and academia. In the governance role, a government deploys and develops regulatory and governance technologies and standards. Based upon the roles, three planning activities are applied. Vertical Mapping is used to answer questions about what to do. Horizontal Mapping is used to answer questions about how to do and what the best practices are. Cognitive Scaling is used to monitor the performance of an interconnected and interactive system composed of several intelligent entities. It is recognized that a country's competitive dynamics and industry structures will change dramatically. Inability to properly plan can lead to permanent loss of competitiveness. It is critical that countries take this transition extremely seriously.

## References

Gray, R. (2017). How long will it take for your job to be automated? BBC. Accessed September 20, 2017. Available at: http://www.bbc.com/capital/story/20170619-how-long-will-it-take-for-your-job-to-be-automated.

Lufkin, B. (2017). Why the biggest challenge facing AI is an ethical one. Accessed September 20, 2017. Available at: http://www.bbc.com/future/story/20170307-the-ethical-challenge-facing-artificial-intelligence.

Mehr, H. (2017). Artificial intelligence: 6 steps government agencies can take. State Scoop. Accessed September 20, 2017. Available at: http://statescoop.com/artificial-intelligence-6-steps-government-agencies-can-take.

PWC (2016). Sizing the prize. PWC's global artificial intelligence study: Exploiting the AI revolution. Accessed September 21, 2017. Available at: https://www.pwc.com/gx/en/issues/data-and-analytics/publications/artificial-intelligence-study.html.

Rao, A. (2017). A strategist's guide to artificial intelligence. Strategy + Business. Accessed September 20, 2017. Available at: https://www.strategy-business.com/article/A-Strategists-Guide-to-Artificial-Intelligence?gko=0abb5&utm_source=itw&utm_medium=20170523&utm_campaign=respB.

# NOTES ON CONTRIBUTORS

**Yongjian Bao** is a tenured professor of policy and strategy with the University of Lethbridge, Canada. His specialization is in the areas of top management team decision-making and industrial innovation. He coauthored seven books on high-tech strategies, crisis management, and peripheral thinking. Dr. Bao was awarded Top Ten Thinkers of Entrepreneurship and Innovation in the year 2016 by Tsinghua Management Review.

**Sergio Biggemann** is a senior lecturer in business marketing at the University of Otago.

**Carlos M. DaSilva** is an associate professor of entrepreneurship at the HEG/HES-SO (University of Applied Sciences), Western Switzerland. He authored the book *Entrepreneurial Finance: A Global Perspective* and works for the Swiss National Innovation Agency (INNOSUISSE) as a lead trainer in the field of entrepreneurship. More at www.carlosdasilva.com.

**Daniel Lemus-Delgado** is professor of theory of international relations of the School of Social Science and Government at Tecnologico de Monterrey. He is member of the National System of Researchers (México). His fields of academic interests are new technologies, international development cooperation, and international relations.

**Nicolas Economou** is the chief executive of H5 and was a pioneer in advocating the application of scientific methods to electronic discovery. He chairs the Law Committees of The Future Society and the IEEE Global Initiative on Ethics of Autonomous and Intelligent Systems and served as chair of the Law Committee of the Global Governance of AI Roundtable hosted in Dubai as part of the annual World Government Summit. He is also a member of the Council on Extended Intelligence (CXI), a joint initiative of the MIT Media Lab and IEEE-SA, and of the American Bar Association's AI Ethics Working

Group. Trained in political science at the Graduate Institute of International Studies of the University of Geneva (Switzerland), he earned his M.B.A. from the Wharton School of Business and chose to forgo completion of his M.P.A. at Harvard's Kennedy School in order to cofound H5.

**Margaret A. Goralski** holds a PhD in international management. She is a professor of strategy at Quinnipiac University in Connecticut. Dr. Goralski is an Albert Schweitzer Fellow; Chapter Chair of Academy of International Business US NE; VP of publications International Academy of Business Disciplines; editor-in-chief of Quarterly Review of Business Disciplines; and UN PRME working group member on sustainability mindset. Current research interests include spirituality and strategic implementation of artificial intelligence, open cognition, and blockchain. Dr. Goralski has authored/edited/coedited multiple journal publications as well as contributing chapters including "Permissionless Evolution of Ethics—Artificial Intelligence" in *Business Strategy in the Artificial Intelligence Economy* with coauthor Krystyna Górniak-Kocikowska.

**Krystyna Górniak-Kocikowska** has a PhD in philosophy from Adam Mickiewicz University in Poznań, Poland, and an MA in religious studies from Temple University. She is a core faculty member at Charter Oak State College; professor emerita of Philosophy at Southern Connecticut State University; member of the Editorial Board of *Journal of Information, Communication & Ethics in Society*; member of the Research Center on Values in Emerging Science and Technology (RC-VEST); and a research fellow at the Albert Schweitzer Institute. Her publications and conference presentations focus mainly on ethical and social issues generated by digital technology, especially Artificial Intelligence; Philosophy of Education; Phenomenology; and Interreligious Dialogue. She has received several research and travel grants (among others, from the EU and from the Kościuszko Foundation).

**Bruce Hedin** is principal scientist at H5, where his focus since 2003 has been on the assessment of the effectiveness of advanced information retrieval technologies, including artificial intelligence, deployed in civil and criminal electronic discovery. In addition to being a frequent speaker and writer on this topic, Dr. Hedin served as a coordinator of US NIST's landmark TREC Legal Track studies on the effectiveness of machine learning and other advanced technologies in electronic discovery (2008–2011). He is also a program committee member of the International Conference on Artificial Intelligence and Law (ICAIL) and a participant in the Sedona Conference's Electronic Document

Retention and Production Working Group (WG1). Dr. Hedin earned his PhD from Stanford University and his B.A. from Cornell University.

**Yolanda Lannquist** is head of Research and Advisory at The Future Society, a nonprofit 'think-and-do-tank' with the mission to advance the responsible adoption of artificial intelligence (AI) and emerging technologies for the benefit of humanity. Yolanda leads projects in AI policy and governance including developing national AI strategies, harnessing AI for Sustainable Development Goals, and mitigating the ethical, safety, and societal impacts of AI. Yolanda has a Master's in Public Policy from Harvard University's Kennedy School of Government and Bachelor's in Economics and European Studies from Columbia University in New York with Phi Beta Kappa honors.

**Armando López-Cuevas** specializes in natural language processing and machine learning. He is professor of the School of Computer Science at Tecnologico de Monterrey. He is member of the Mexican Academy of Computing and the National System of Researchers in México.

**Nicholas Miailhe** cofounded The Future Society in 2014 and incubated it at the Harvard Kennedy School of Government. The think-and-do tank specializes in questions of impact and governance of emerging technologies, starting with Artificial Intelligence through its AI Initiative. A recognized thought-leader, strategist, and implementer, Nicolas advises governments, international organizations, NGOs, and industrial players across Europe, America, and Asia. Nicolas is a member of the OECD High-Level Expert Group on AI Governance and of the Global Council on Extended Intelligence (IEEE and MIT Media Lab). He teaches at Sciences Po Paris, is a visiting professor at the IE School of Global & Public Affairs in Madrid and at the Dubai School of Government. Nicolas is also a senior visiting research fellow with the Program on Science, Technology and Society at Harvard Kennedy School and a fellow with the Center for the Governance of Change at IE Business School in Madrid.

**J. Mark Munoz** is a professor of international business at Millikin University in Illinois and a former visiting fellow at the Kennedy School of Government at Harvard University. He is a recipient of several awards including four Best Research Paper Awards, an international book award, a literary award, and the ACBSP Teaching Excellence Award, among others. Aside from top-tier journal publications, he has authored/edited/coedited 14 books such as: *Winning Across Borders, International Social Entrepreneurship, Contemporary*

*Microenterprises: Concepts and Cases, Handbook on the Geopolitics of Business, Managerial Forensics, Advances in Geoeconomics,* and *Global Business Intelligence.*

**Al Naqvi**, the pioneer of the field of Enterprise Artificial Intelligence, developed the first and most comprehensive body of knowledge (and courses) for AI in Corporate Strategy, AI in Finance, AI in Marketing, AI in HR, AI in Competitive Intelligence, AI in CSR, Deep Learning, AI in Supply Chain Management. The courses developed by Professor Naqvi are now offered by leading universities. His work has been recognized by world's leading professional societies, universities, and companies. Over 300 companies have benefited from Naqvi's research. He is widely published in both academic and practitioner publications. Al Naqvi's professional research interests are broad and include artificial intelligence, applied AI, robotic process automation, deep learning, complex adaptive systems, cognitive organizations and leadership, and strategic cognitive transformation. He teaches several classes on Applied Artificial Intelligence, Deep Learning, RPA, and Cognitive Transformation at the American Institute of Artificial Intelligence. Professor Naqvi is passionate about teaching people about the potential and practical applications of artificial intelligence. He calls it reskilling and re-intellectualization of the workforce. He is the editor of the *Journal of Artificial Intelligence in Business, Policy, and Economy.* He is a leading expert in transforming companies from the "e" to the "AI" era. He specializes in total and integrated business transformation by using artificial intelligence. He has designed several products using Deep Neural Networks. Known for making artificial intelligence fun and easy to understand, he has appeared in various conferences and shows all over the world. He lives in the greater Washington, DC, area.

**Oleksiy Osiyevskyy** is an assistant professor of entrepreneurship and innovation in the University of Calgary, with background education and experience in the development of complex software systems. In his management scholarship, Oleksiy concentrates on the problems of achieving and sustaining firm growth through successfully engaging in high-tech entrepreneurial strategies. Particular areas of expertise include analyzing and designing innovative business models, improving the efficiency and effectiveness of corporate innovation practices, and evidence-based strategies for developing high-growth new ventures.

**Jean-Marc Rickli** is the head of global risk and resilience at the Geneva Centre for Security Policy (GCSP) in Geneva, Switzerland. He is also a research fellow at King's College London, a nonresident fellow in modern warfare and security at TRENDS Research and Advisory in Abu Dhabi. He is a senior advisor for the AI (Artificial Intelligence) Initiative at The Future Society at Harvard Kennedy School and an expert on autonomous weapons systems for the United Nations and for the United Nations Institute for Disarmament and Research (UNIDIR). Dr. Rickli received his PhD and M.Phil. in International Relations from Oxford University, UK, where he was also a Berrow scholar at Lincoln College.

**Luis Soto** is a systems engineer, entrepreneur, and Latin-American guru in artificial intelligence and expert systems.

**Melodena Stephens** is professor of innovation management at the Mohammed Bin Rashid School of Government. She has over 25 years of corporate and academic working experience. She worked and lived in India, UAE, Taiwan, the United States, and Germany. She consults and researches in the field of strategy and public policy, specifically impact valuation, entrepreneurship, and place branding.

**Dirk Nicolas Wagner** is dean of the faculty of Business Economics & Management and professor of strategic management at Karlshochschule International University (GER). He studied economics and management at Université de Fribourg (CH) and Royal Holloway University of London (UK), graduating as a MBA in International Management and Dr.rer.pol. in the area of New Institutional Economics. Since the 1990s, he has been dealing with questions related to man and machine governance and he regularly publishes with the Zukunftsinstitut in Frankfurt a.M. Prior to joining Karlshochschule, he served in various senior management and board member positions in the technical services industry in Europe.

**Nathalie de Marcellis-Warin** is full professor at Polytechnique Montreal, Department of Mathematics and Industrial Engineering. She is president and chief executive officer at CIRANO, an interuniversity center of research, liaison, and transfer of knowledge on Public Policy and Risk Management encompassing 11 universities as well as more than 230 affiliated researchers and 20 key partners (government and business), and a Visiting Scholar at Harvard T. Chan School of Public Health. Her research interests are Risk Management and Decision Theory in risk and uncertainty, using Data Science and Nonstructured Data.

**Thierry Warin** is a full professor at SKEMA Business School and director of the SKEMA AI Global Lab. A faculty affiliate at the MOC Network at the Harvard Business School since 2016, he is an alumnus of the Salzburg Global Seminar, a former visiting scholar at the Minda De Gunzburg Center for European Studies (Harvard University, 2005) and the Weatherhead Center for International Affairs at Harvard University in 2015–17. His research is mainly on Data Science in Finance and International Economics.

# INDEX

Page numbers in *italics* and **bold** denote figures and tables, respectively.

9 781785 274954